PRAISE FOR 7 [barcode] P9-ECO-046

Hamilton Helmer is the best kind of big thinker—he offers great insights that you can turn into real world action. At Spotify the 7 Powers are widely used as we discuss new initiatives. His distillation of the key types of strategic power, how to find them, how to leverage them, and how to maintain them is a fantastic toolset for companies at every stage.

DANIEL EK, CEO AND CO-FOUNDER OF SPOTIFY

The forces of competition are just incredibly strong. Everyone is trying to eat your lunch, and if you don't read 7 Powers *you're going to die a lot sooner.*

REED HASTINGS, CEO AND CO-FOUNDER OF NETFLIX

7 Powers *lays out a clear, compelling and insightful framework for thinking about the persistent sources of competitive advantage. Helmer draws on three decades of experience to break down how companies establish power and shape their industries, illustrating at every turn with entertaining and illuminating examples.*

JONATHAN LEVIN, PHILIP H KNIGHT DEAN, STANFORD GRADUATE SCHOOL OF BUSINESS

Hamilton Helmer understands that strategy starts with invention. He can't tell you what to invent, but he can and does show what it takes for a new invention to become a valuable business.

PETER THIEL, ENTREPRENEUR AND INVESTOR

7 Powers *provides vital guidance for any businessperson developing strategy. I have known Hamilton for more than a decade since his time as a strategy advisor to Adobe, and I am delighted that he is now sharing his original and compelling business insights.*

BRUCE CHIZEN, FORMER CEO OF ADOBE

Hamilton is a deep thinker who makes a compelling connection between passion and good business. His ideas are well thought out, wise, and often challenging. I always look forward to what he has to say.

PETE DOCTER, PIXAR DIRECTOR AND TWO-TIME ACADEMY AWARD WINNER FOR *UP* AND *INSIDE OUT*

Making a small number of decisions wisely is far more important than making a lot of decisions correctly. Hamilton Helmer explains exactly how the leaders of the world's most successful businesses get that small number just right.

MIKE MORITZ, CHAIRMAN OF SEQUOIA CAPITAL

7 Powers

The Foundations of Business Strategy

Hamilton Helmer
Foreword by Reed Hastings

7 Powers: The Foundations of Business Strategy

For information about this title or to order other books and/or electronic media, contact the publisher:
Deep Strategy LLC
1 First Street, Los Altos, CA 94022
7powers.com

ISBNs: 978-0-9981163-0-3 (Hardbound)
        978-0-9981163-1-0 (Paperback)
        978-0-9981163-2-7 (Kindle)

Printed in the United States of America

Cover and Interior design: Irene Young and Carol Ehrlich

TABLE OF CONTENTS

FOREWORD

BY REED HASTINGS

Hard to imagine, but my relationship with Hamilton began purely as a courtesy. Among the many entries on my calendar for Sept. 29, 2004 was a visit from him and Larry Tint, founders of Strategy Capital, a hedge fund investor in Netflix. At that time Netflix was a small DVD-by-mail rental company, and we had only gone public two and a half years before.

Typically, in meetings of this type, investors will suss out management, probe for additional color on the company. They are kicking the tires, in other words. But Hamilton and Larry took this sit-down in an entirely—and refreshingly—unexpected direction. Hamilton started with a crisp overview of Power Dynamics, his novel strategy framework, and then utilized that very framework to offer up a penetrating assessment of Netflix's strategic imperatives. Incisive, extraordinary. The meeting quickly became anything but a courtesy.

Hamilton's impressions stuck with me, and a half-decade later they percolated into an idea. By that point, in 2009, the existential threat from Blockbuster was behind us, and we were on track to reach almost $1.7 billion in sales. These were hard-won advances, but even so our strategy challenges were no less daunting. The clock was ticking on our red envelope business, as DVDs by mail was clearly a transitional technology. And looming was the prospect of facing off against huge competitors with resources far beyond ours: Google, Amazon, Time Warner and Apple to name several.

As I had learned over my years as a businessperson, strategy is an unusual beast. Most of my time and that of everyone else at Netflix must be spent achieving superb execution. Fail at this, and you will surely stumble. Sadly, though, such execution alone will not ensure success. If you don't get your strategy right, you are at risk. I have been around long enough that I remember the lesson of the IBM PC. Here was a breakthrough product—the customer take-up was amazing: 40,000 upon announcement of the product and more than 100,000 in its first year. No one had ever seen anything like it. IBM's execution was flawless. Their superb management never missed a beat. It would be hard to imagine another company at that time scaling physical production as rapidly as they did without tripping up. Even their marketing was inspired. Remember Charlie Chaplin as the friendly face of their campaign, welcoming all of us to the new world of computing?

But they got the strategy wrong. By outsourcing the OS and permitting Microsoft to sell it to others, IBM squandered their opportunity for the kind of network economy home run that had powered their mainframe juggernaut, System 360. Then their decision to outsource the microprocessor to Intel, while still promoting applications hard-wired to it, likewise ceded yet another important front. As a consequence, they sealed the fate of the PC, rendering it an unattractive box-assembly business. Try as they might, they could never right this ship. The inevitable denouement came with their 2005 fire sale of the business to Lenovo.

But rewind to my 2009 problem. The question facing me was this: How could we energetically pursue thoughtful strategizing at Netflix? Fortunately, by this time, we had expended a great deal of effort honing our unique culture—and that provided the key. We could face up to our challenging strategic climate by tapping into the very values we had worked so hard to embed in the company.

Our first public "culture deck," released in August of 2009, identified nine highly valued behaviors. The first was "Judgment." As we elaborated:

- You make wise decisions … despite ambiguity

- You identify root causes and get beyond treating symptoms

- You think strategically and can articulate what you are *and are not* trying to do

- You smartly separate what must be done well now and what can be improved later

Wisdom, root causes, thinking strategically, smart prioritization—it made sense to me that all of this mapped to strategy. But to remain true to our culture, senior management could not simply impose its own view of strategy. Instead we had to develop in our people an understanding of the levers of strategy so that, on their own, they could flexibly apply this to their work. Only in this way could we honor another of the pillars of our culture: managing through context, not control.

This perspective, however, created a dilemma for me. Strategy is a complex subject—how could this "context" be learned by our people expeditiously? Having held a lifelong interest in education, I have always been much taken with an anecdote concerning the Nobel laureate physicist Richard Feynman, as recounted by James Gleick in his book *Genius*. Professor Feynman, one of the truly great science teachers of his time, was asked to do a lecture on a difficult area of Quantum Mechanics. Feynman agreed but then several days later recanted, saying "You know I couldn't do it...That means we really don't understand it."

In the very same way, our challenge around strategy was clear: did anyone "really understand it" enough to teach it? Fortunately, I recalled the succinctness with which Hamilton summarized strategy in his 2004 presentation. I initiated a dialog with Hamilton and grew more and more convinced of his unique qualifications. In the end, Hamilton developed a program which conveyed to a large number of Netflix's key people a fundamental understanding of strategy. This effort was a huge success. Still today, many Netflixers look back on it as one of the best educational experiences of their professional lives.

Hamilton is so much more than an able synthesizer and communicator, as *7 Powers* demonstrates. Any strategy framework, to be broadly useful to a businessperson, must address *all* the key strategy issues facing an organization. Hamilton has long been aware of the deficiencies in existing frameworks. His solution? To forge ahead with entirely novel conceptual advances, and then to bind these together into a unified whole. Let me give you two examples of such advances from *7 Powers* which stand out for me:

- *Counter-Positioning.* Throughout my business career I have often observed powerful incumbents, once lauded for their business acumen, failing to adjust to a new competitive reality. The result is always a stunning fall from grace. A superficial thinker might pin this on lack of vision and leadership. Not Hamilton. By inventing the concept of Counter-Positioning, he was able to peel back the layers to peer into the deeper reality of these situations. Rather than lacking vision, Hamilton established, these incumbents are in fact acting in an entirely predictable and economically rational way. Our earlier battle with Blockbuster bore out this notion.

- *Power Progression.* At Netflix, we aggressively prioritize our attention in order to focus on what is essential to accomplish now. This applies to strategy as well: what are the near-in strategic imperatives? Unfortunately, existing strategy frameworks offered little guidance. There was recognition that this was an important issue, but none of those other frameworks could address it in a systematic, reliable, sufficiently transparent way. How did Hamilton respond to this void? Over a span of decades, he developed and refined the Power Progression, illustrating the approximate time fuse for each of the competitive battles facing a business person. It's an extraordinary advance in the usefulness of strategic thinking.

These two advances in understanding are essential for getting to the root of a broad swath of strategy challenges. They are just some of the fruits of my association with Hamilton. Now it's you who's in for a treat. *7 Powers* tightly integrates the numerous insights he has developed in his several decades of consulting, active equity investing and teaching. It is a uniquely clear and comprehensive distillation of strategy. It will change how you think about business and pull into focus your critical strategy challenges, not to mention their solutions. It may not be the lightest of beach reads; you probably won't tear through it in a night, but I am confident that your attention will be rewarded many times over.

— Reed Hastings
CEO and Co-Founder of Netflix

*This book is dedicated to my
family—the joy of my life*

INTRODUCTION

The Strategy Compass

The arc of any celebrated business is underpinned by decisive strategy choices that are few and typically made amidst the profound uncertainty of rapid change. Get these crux choices wrong and you face a future of persistent pain, or even outright failure. To get them right, you must constantly attune your strategy to unfolding circumstances—ponderous planning cycles or handoffs to outside experts won't get you there.

This reality begs the question, "Can the intellectual discipline of Strategy make a difference in such adaptation?" After decades as a business advisor, active equity investor and teacher, my conclusion is, "Yes it can." But with this hard-won conclusion comes a caveat informed by Pasteur's well-known dictum: "Chance only favors the prepared mind." Strategy serves best not as an analytical redoubt, but rather in developing the "prepared mind" of those on the ground.

To fulfill this role as a real-time strategy compass, a Strategy framework must be "simple but not simplistic." If not simple, then concepts cannot be easily retained for day-to-day reference—usefulness is lost. If simplistic, then you risk missing something crucial. Easier said than done, though. For a subject as complex as Strategy, "simple but not simplistic" is a high hurdle.

Thanks to Bill Bain's openness to an oddball like me, I was privileged to start my Strategy career right out of graduate school at Bain & Company in 1978. Professor Michael Porter hadn't yet published his landmark book *Competitive Strategy*, and BCG and Bain & Company were in overdrive, embedding a Strategy sensibility in the corporate world, and in the process building two of the most respected brands in management consulting. In the decades since, Strategy as a discipline has made enormous strides, both theoretically and empirically. Even so, current Strategy frameworks are not up to the challenge of "simple but not simplistic." The simple ones are too simplistic, and those less simplistic are still not simple.

The 7 Powers, a Strategy framework borne of hundreds of consulting engagements and decades of active equity investing, clears this hurdle. Because it covers all attractive strategic positions, it is not simplistic, while its unitary focus on Power makes it sufficiently simple to be learned, retained and used by any businessperson. It can be, and indeed has been, successfully employed inside businesses as a shared, actionable understanding of the primary levers of Strategy. If your business does not have at least one of these seven Power types, then you lack a viable strategy, and you are vulnerable.

My goal in writing this book is to enable you to flexibly navigate the hazardous shoals of strategy development. I am not offering you specific advice for your individual business; rather I am giving you a lens through which to see your strategic landscape. This lens will bring into high relief the critical strategy challenges you must solve. But here's the irony: only by dealing in theory can this book be of most practical value.

If you read this book and internalize the 7 Powers, you will have the "prepared mind" referenced by Pasteur and be ready to identify, create and seize an opportunity for Power in those rare formative moments. The success of your business depends on it.

"Not Simplistic" First

We will now begin our Strategy journey together. When we are done, you will be fluent in the 7 Powers. This will empower you by putting at your fingertips a workable understanding of Strategy to guide you in those crucial high-flux moments that will define your business.

Making the right decisions in these moments has enormous payback. This high return, however, is matched with the high hurdle discussed above: to be a useful such cognitive guide, the precepts of Strategy must be distilled to a framework that is simple but not simplistic.

To gain your confidence that the 7 Powers clears this hurdle I will, in this Introduction, detail how Power is the deep driver of potential fundamental business value. This formally articulated connection will give you assurance that what follows in the rest of the book is comprehensive, another word for "not simplistic." The seven ensuing chapters, each on one Power type, will build on this foundation to fashion the 7 Powers. My experience with many business-people is that the resulting construct is sufficiently "simple" to serve this role of an ongoing strategy compass.

My jumping-off point will be a brief look at Intel, one of the most important companies to come out of Silicon Valley, my home turf. Intel is an especially telling case because, as we will see, it is one of those rare instances of dramatic success mirrored by an equally dramatic failure. This uncommon intersection allows us to isolate success drivers. I will use this to define Power, the central concept of this book, as well as Strategy (the intellectual discipline) and strategy (the specific approach of a single business).

Intel Hits the Mother Lode

To grasp the phenomenal success of Intel, let's first rewind nearly five decades to Silicon Valley's inceptive moment. There, in 1968, Robert Noyce and Gordon Moore, fed up with the strictures of corporate parent Fairchild Camera and Instrument, cut ties with Fairchild Semiconductor to found Intel[1] in Santa Clara, California. Intel went on to develop the first microprocessor, a seminal moment for personal computers and servers, as well as the numerous ubiquitous technologies they now sustain: the Internet, search, social media and digital entertainment. Without Intel, we would have no Google, Facebook, Netflix, Uber, Alibaba, Oracle or Microsoft. Modern society, in short, would not exist.

To our modern ears, the very name—Intel—rings with success. Over nearly half a century, Noyce and Moore's humble startup has ascended to become the undisputed leader in microprocessors, boasting some $50B in revenues and a market cap of around $150B—a phenomenal success by any measure.

But how and why do successes like this take wing? The field of Strategy examines precisely that question. To define it more formally:

Strategy: *the study of the fundamental determinants of potential business value*

The objective here is both positive—to reveal the foundations of business value—and normative—to guide businesspeople in their own value-creation efforts.

Following a line of reasoning common in Economics, Strategy can be usefully separated into two topics:

- *Statics—i.e. "Being There"*: what makes Intel's microprocessor business so durably valuable?

- *Dynamics—i.e. "Getting There"*: what developments yielded this attractive state of affairs in the first place?

These two form the core of the discipline of Strategy, and though interwoven, they lead to quite different, although highly complementary, lines of inquiry. As such, they will comprise the subject matter of Part I and Part II of this book.

For now, though, let's return to our case study of Intel. Their defining success came in microprocessors—the brains of today's computers. But, perhaps surprisingly, Intel did not start out in that business. Their initial thrust was into computer memories, and indeed they styled themselves "The Memory Company." The invention of microprocessors came about only as an offshoot of a development job for Busicom, a Japanese calculator company. Their motivation in taking this on was simply to generate much needed cash for their memories business. After a long gestation period, though, microprocessors gained traction, and the paths of their two businesses diverged, leading to wildly different value outcomes: $0 for memories and $150B for microprocessors.

All of this begs the question, "Why did Intel succeed in microprocessors but fail in memories?" Both enjoyed numerous shared advantages. Intel was first mover in each market, for instance, and both were large, fast-growth semiconductor businesses, each enjoying the considerable benefits of Intel's managerial, technical and financial prowess. Without question, then, the explanation must lie outside the bounds of all common ground shared between memories and microprocessors. So what's the answer? Why did one succeed and the other fail?

I am an economist, and with that comes a healthy respect for the arbitraging force of competition. Intel's retreat and eventual exit from memories reflects this force perfectly. Intel's great leadership, their superb business practices—none of it could offer any refuge. Yet somehow microprocessors escaped this fate—there was something different about this business. It eluded such arbitrage, enabling Intel to continue earning the very attractive returns that underlie their stock price today. It wasn't for lack of competition, either. The competitive assault in microprocessors has, over the decades, been at least as intense as that in memories: IBM, Motorola, AMD, Zilog, National Semiconductor, ARM, NEC, TI and countless others have poured billions into this business.

We can only assume microprocessors possessed some sort of rare characteristics which materially improved cash flow, while simultaneously inhibiting competitive arbitrage. I refer to these as **Power**.[2]

Power: the set of conditions creating the potential
for persistent differential returns

Power is the core concept of Strategy and of this book, too. It is the Holy Grail of business—notoriously difficult to reach, but well worth your attention and study. And so it is the task of this book to detail the specific conditions that result in Power (Part I: Statics) and how to attain them (Part II: Dynamics).

The Mantra[3]

For Intel, microprocessors had Power and memories did not, and this made all the difference. Intel's enduring triple-digit billion market cap reflects this Power applied across a large revenue stream. Such an outcome is the goal of any business and this allows me to define strategy (a company's strategy) in the following way:

strategy: a route to continuing Power
in significant markets

I refer to this as The Mantra, since it provides an exhaustive characterization of the requirements of a strategy.

But despite the comprehensive nature of The Mantra, I have also considerably narrowed the definition of strategy. The term, in business, has become ubiquitous. Searching Google Scholar for articles about "strategy" yields a mind-numbing 5,150,000 hits. Over the last several decades business thinkers and corporate problem-solvers have developed an inclination to elevate nearly any problem to higher status by affixing "strategy" or "strategic," hence "strategic suppliers," "customer strategy," "organizational strategy" and even "strategic planning." There is nothing intrinsically incorrect about these uses, but my thinking cuts a different way. Decades of teaching and practice have convinced me that by adopting a heterodox, narrower view of Strategy and strategy, we gain considerable conceptual clarity and substantially enhance the usefulness of the concepts. In this instance, less is more.

Two additional clarifications are needed to narrow our discussion of "Strategy" and "strategy." First, though Game Theory has important intersections with Strategy—the whole notion of arbitrage, for example, can be likened to the process of players playing their best games over time—Game Theory's definition of strategy simply refers to the set of actions available to a player and thus proves far more inclusive than my definition. Even an optimal strategy in Game Theory, such as a Nash Equilibrium, implies no assurance of value creation. Intel's retreat and exit from memories would have appeared optimal through a Game Theory lens—but no route to Power resulted. If we hold the ultimate normative benchmark in business to be value creation, then Game Theory alone is not sufficiently constrained to provide a normative framework for Strategy.[4]

Second, my definitions are distanced from the school of thought which centers on cleverness in choices—the idea that if you read Sun Tzu or hire a prestigious consulting firm, you can somehow make lemonade out of lemons. I have ignored this mindset on purpose. Businesspeople are usually smart, motivated, well-informed; with established businesses, this sort of cleverness typically figures into the perpetual to and fro of arbitrage—it's necessary for value creation, sure, but relatively common and hardly sufficient.

Value

So far in this chapter I have separately defined "Strategy" and "strategy." The first tied back to value, the second to Power.

As an Economist it is my habit to use some light math to bring clarity to such definitions. In what follows, I establish the link between "Strategy" and "strategy" by mapping value to my definition of strategy.

For the purposes of this book, "value" refers to absolute fundamental shareholder value[5]—the ongoing enterprise value shareholders attribute to the strategically separate business of an individual firm. The best proxy for this is the net present value (NPV) of expected future free cash flow (FCF) of that activity.[6]

$$NPV = \Sigma(CF_i/[1+d]^i)$$

Where:

$CF_i \equiv$ expected free cash flow in period i

$d \equiv$ discount rate

A mathematically equivalent[7] but more felicitous formula for the NPV of free cash flow is:

$$NPV = M_0\, g\, \bar{s}\, \bar{m}$$

Where:

$M_0 \equiv$ current market size

$g \equiv$ discounted market growth factor

$\bar{s} \equiv$ long-term market share

$\bar{m} \equiv$ long-term differential margin (net profit margin in excess of that needed to cover the cost of capital)

So:

$$\boxed{\text{Value} = M_0\, g\, \bar{s}\, \bar{m}}$$

I refer to this as the **Fundamental Equation of Strategy.** Recall my definition of strategy:

strategy: a route to continuing Power
in significant markets

The product of M_0 and g reflect market scale over time; hence they capture the "significant markets" component of this definition. The impact of competitive arbitrage is expressed in margins and market share simultaneously, so the maintenance or increase of s market share,[8] while maintaining a positive and material long-term differential margin, provides the numerical expression of Power. In other words, put another way:

Potential Value = [Market Scale] * [Power]

This is potential value and operational excellence is required to achieve that potential. Examining Intel through this lens, we can identify a large-scale market ($M_0 g$) for both memories and microprocessors. So what accounted for the utterly different value outcome? Under Andy Grove, operational excellence was the norm, so it was Power that made the difference: over time competitive arbitrage drove $\overline{m}$ in memories negative, whereas Power enabled Intel to maintain a high and positive $\overline{m}$ in microprocessors.[9]

Upcoming Topics

This simple math confirms my strategy definition as an exhaustive statement of value. Moreover, it's normative as well. Fulfill the imperatives of "The Mantra" and you will create business value. Importantly, too, it is inclusive of both Statics and Dynamics.

That said, you may not yet find my strategy definition satisfying, because it tells you nothing beyond the math of the Fundamental Equation; so far it is completely agnostic as to exactly what sorts of conditions have a high probability of fostering durable differential returns. That is the objective of the 7 Powers framework and the chapters to follow, the meat and potatoes of this book. Before I can make The Mantra operationally meaningful, I must identify and detail the specific types of Power and how they come to be.

To conclude, let me debut some themes that will recur in the chapters to come:

- *Persistence.* The Fundamental Formula of Strategy specifies unchanging m—differential margins. Anyone who has done valuation work, M&A or value investing knows well that the bulk of a business' value comes in the out years. For faster-growing companies, this reality becomes more accentuated. You won't yield much from a few good years of positive *m* which then tapers off or disappears altogether. For example, let's use a common valuation model: if a company were growing at 10% per year, the next three years would account for only about 15% of its value.

Remember, we've reserved the term "Power" for those conditions that create *durable* differential returns. In other words, we are trying to discern long-term competitive equilibria, not just next year's results. Intel's current $150B market cap reflects not only investors' expectations of high returns but also those which continue for a *very long time.* Thus persistence proves a key feature in this value focus, and such persistence requires that any theory of Strategy is a dynamic equilibrium theory—it's all about establishing and *maintaining* an unassailable perch. Strategy requires you identify and develop those rare conditions which produce a value sinecure immune to competitive onslaught. Intel eventually achieved this in microprocessors but could never get there in memories.

Briefly: a digression, but a vital one. Let me comment on the popular misperception that the stock market cares only about *this* quarter's results. It is especially pertinent to our discussion of persistence, because if this assumption were true, then we could discount any talk of persistence altogether. However, over the longer term—that is, ignoring speculative perturbations—investors are aware of the 10%/15% calculation I mentioned above, and this is what drives analysts' value models—they are attuned to their expectation of free cash-generation over the longer term. Of course, changes in current performance may result in significant recalibrations of their expectations, but this is not because they only care about the short-term; rather it is because current performance is a significant indicator of future performance and hence shapes long-term expectations. For those long-term expectations to bear out, though, persistence remains key.

- *Dual Attributes.* Power is as hard to achieve as it is important. As stated above, its defining feature *ex post* is persistent differential returns. Accordingly, we must associate it with both *magnitude* and *duration.*

  1. *Benefit.* The conditions created by Power must materially augment cash flow, and this is the magnitude aspect of our dual attributes. It can manifest as any combination of increased prices, reduced costs and/or lessened investment needs.

  2. *Barrier.* The Benefit must not only augment cash flow, but it must persist, too. There must be some aspect of the Power conditions which prevents existing and potential competitors, both direct and functional, from engaging in the sort of value-destroying arbitrage Intel experienced with its memory business. This is the duration aspect of Power

  As I delineate the seven types of Power in the chapters to come, I will similarly describe their unique Benefit/Barrier combination. The Benefit conditions probably won't sound all too rare—they are met often in business. Indeed, every major cost-cutting initiative qualifies. The Barrier conditions, on the other hand, prove far rarer, a reality that merely proves the ubiquity of competitive arbitrage. As a strategist, then, my advice is, "Always look to the Barrier first." In Intel's case, the heart of its microprocessors strategy can be best understood not by sorting through the multiplicity of Intel's value improvements, but by deducing why decades of capable and committed competition failed to emulate or undermine those improvements.

- *Industry Economics and Competitive Position.* The conditions of Power involve the interaction between the underlying industry's economics and the specific business' competitive position. In Part I, I will parse these two drivers for each of the seven types of Power analyzed. This adds an explicitness that is useful in understanding and applying the concepts developed, while also shedding light on the role of "industry attractiveness" in creating value potential.

- *Complex Competition.* Power, unlike strength, is an explicitly relative concept: it is about your strength in relation to that of a *specific* competitor. Good strategy involves assessing Power with respect to each competitor, which includes potential as well as existing competitors, and functional as well as direct competitors. Any such players could be the source of the arbitrage you are trying to circumvent, and any one arbitrageur is enough to drive down differential margins.[10]

- *Single Business Focus.* The protagonist of Strategy and of a strategy is each strategically separate business by itself, even if they exist within the same corporation, a common occurrence. In the case of Intel, memories and microprocessors were essentially separate businesses, posing two unique orthogonal Strategy problems. The concept of Power also takes into account this separation. The special considerations arising from the interplay of multiple businesses under a single corporate roof is the subject matter of Corporate Strategy. This is beyond the scope of the current edition of this book.[11] I hope to address that in later editions, as the tools of Power Dynamics yield useful insights.

- *Leadership.* The notion of Power (and the impact of its lack) is what underlies Warren Buffett's view that if you combine a poor business with a good manager, it is not the business that loses its reputation. On the other hand, always the domain of Economists, I am a strong believer in the importance of leadership in the creation of value. Intel's experience is again instructive. I have little doubt that the managerial acuity of Bob Noyce, Gordon Moore and Andy Grove would be remembered quite differently had they stuck with memories. True, but it is also true that their combined leadership was decisive in backing microprocessors in the first place and in a variety of choices that assured "a route to continuing Power." These contrasting assessments of the contribution of leadership hint at the differences between Dynamics and Statics, a difference I will address explicitly in chapters to come.

Conclusion

My many years of advising companies and making value-driven equity bets has made it crystal clear to me that the ascent of great companies is not linear but more a step function. There are critical moments when decisions are made that inexorably shape the company's future trajectory. To get these crux moves right, you must flexibly adapt your strategy to emerging circumstances. The goal of this book is ambitious: to enable such flexibility by making the discipline of Strategy relevant to you in those high-flux formative moments. But standing in the way is a daunting challenge: the core concepts of Strategy must be distilled into a framework that is simple but not simplistic. Only then can it serve you as such a real-time cognitive guide.

This Introduction formally deduces definitions of Power, strategy and Strategy from the determinants of business value. This one-to-one mapping assures that major business objectives are not overlooked. This is what "not simplistic" means.[12]

This then creates a firm foundation for the seven following chapters, each devoted to one of the 7 Powers. Having worked your way through those and digested the mnemonics developed, you can then judge for yourself whether "simple," the other side of this phrase, has been achieved. I can say this: many business people have used and are using the 7 Powers and have found it sufficiently memorable to be easily referenced day-to-day. I hope you have the same experience and that this book can assist you in building a great company.

Appendix to Introduction: Derivation of the Fundamental Equation of Strategy

Definitions

$\pi_i \equiv Profits\ in\ period\ i\ (after\ taxes, before\ interest)$

$I_i \equiv Net\ investment\ in\ period\ i$

$\quad = \Delta\ Working\ Capital + Gross\ fixed\ investment - Depreciation$

$K_i \equiv Capital\ at\ end\ of\ period\ i$

$K_0 \equiv Initial\ capital$

$P \equiv Terminal\ Sale\ Price$

$c \equiv Cost\ of\ capital$

$r \equiv Rate\ of\ return$

$\gamma \equiv Differential\ return = r - c$

$\eta \equiv Top\ line\ growth$

$CF_i \equiv Cash\ flow\ in\ period\ i = \pi_i - I_i$

Net Present Value

$$NPV = -K_0 + \sum_{i=1}^{i=n} \frac{\pi_i - I_i}{(1+c)^i} + \frac{P}{(1+c)^n}$$

$$= -K_0 + \sum_{i=1}^{i=n} \frac{\pi_i - (K_i - K_{i-1})}{(1+c)^i} + \frac{P}{(1+c)^n}$$

$$= -\text{Initial investment} + \text{Discounted cash flows} + \text{Discounted terminal value}$$

$$= \sum_{i=1}^{i=n} \frac{\pi_i}{(1+c)^i} - K_0 + \sum_{i=1}^{i=n} \frac{-(K_i - K_{i-1})}{(1+c)^i} + \frac{P}{(1+c)^n}$$

$$= \sum_{i=1}^{i=n} \frac{\pi_i}{(1+c)^i} - \left[K_0 + \sum_{i=1}^{i=n} \frac{-(K_i - K_{i-1})}{(1+c)^i} \right] + \frac{P}{(1+c)^n}$$

Simplifying the Middle Term

$$K_0 + \sum_{i=1}^{i=n} \frac{(K_i - K_{i-1})}{(1+c)^i} = K_0 + \frac{K_1 - K_0}{(1+c)} + \frac{K_2 - K_1}{(1+c)^2} + \cdots + \frac{K_n - K_{n+1}}{(1+c)^n}$$

$$= K_0 - \frac{K_0}{(1+c)} + \frac{K_1}{(1+c)} - \frac{K_1}{(1+c)^2} + \frac{K_2}{(1+c)^2} - \cdots + \frac{K_{n-1}}{(1+c)^{n-1}} - \frac{K_{n-1}}{(1+c)^n} + \frac{K_n}{(1+c)^n}$$

$$= K_0\left(1 - \frac{1}{1+c}\right) + K_1\left(\frac{1}{1+c} - \frac{1}{(1+c)^2}\right) + \cdots + K_{n-1}\left(\frac{1}{(1+c)^{n-1}} - \frac{1}{(1+c)^n}\right) + \frac{K_n}{(1+c)^n}$$

$$= \frac{K_0}{(1+c)^0}\left(1 - \frac{1}{1+c}\right) + \frac{K_1}{(1+c)^1}\left(1 - \frac{1}{1+c}\right) + \cdots + \frac{K_{n-1}}{(1+c)^{n-1}}\left(1 - \frac{1}{1+c}\right) + \frac{K_n}{(1+c)^n}$$

$$= \frac{K_0}{(1+c)^0}\left(\frac{1}{1+c}\right) + \frac{K_1}{(1+c)^1}\left(\frac{1}{1+c}\right) + \cdots + \frac{K_{n-1}}{(1+c)^{n-1}}\left(\frac{1}{1+c}\right) + \frac{K_n}{(1+c)^n}$$

$$= K_0\frac{c}{1+c} + K_1\frac{c}{(1+c)^2} + \cdots + K_{n-1}\frac{c}{(1+c)^n} + \frac{K_n}{(1+c)^n}$$

$$= \sum_{i=1}^{i=n} K_{i-1}\frac{c}{(1+c)^i} + \frac{K_n}{(1+c)^n} \qquad \boxed{\text{This is the simplified middle term. Substituting this back:}}$$

$$\Rightarrow NPV = \sum_{i=1}^{i=n} \frac{\pi_i}{(1+c)^i} - \left[\sum_{i=1}^{i=n} K_{i-1}\frac{c}{(1+c)^i} + \frac{K_n}{(1+c)^n}\right] + \frac{P}{(1+c)^n}$$

$$= \sum_{i=1}^{i=n} K_{i-1}\frac{\pi_i - cK_{i-1}}{(1+c)^i} + \frac{P - K_n}{(1+c)^n}$$

Assume the business has a finite life = L. At t = L, P = 0. So $\exists$ an n* < L $\ni$ $|P - K_n| < \epsilon$ with an ϵ that is not material to NPV. Thus at n* we can ignore the second term $\frac{P-K_n}{(1+c)^n}$. Thus

$$NPV = \sum_{i=1}^{i=n*} K_{i-1}\frac{\pi_i - cK_{i-1}}{(1+c)^i}$$

$$= \sum_{i=1}^{i=n*} \frac{rK_{i-1} - cK_{i-1}}{(1+c)^i}$$

$$= \sum_{i=1}^{i=n*} \frac{K_{i-1}(r - c)}{(1+c)^i}$$

$$= \sum_{i=1}^{i=n*} \frac{K_{i-1}\gamma}{(1+c)^i}$$

$$= \sum_{i=1}^{i=n*} \frac{K_0(1+\eta)^{i+1}}{(1+c)^i}\gamma$$

$$= K_0\sum_{i=1}^{i=n*} \frac{(1+\eta)^{i+1}}{(1+c)^i}\gamma$$

$$\Rightarrow NPV = K_0 g\gamma \qquad where\ g \equiv the\ discounted\ growth\ factor = \sum_{i=1}^{i=n*} \frac{(1+\eta)^{i+1}}{(1+c)^i}$$

First-period profits in excess of their capital cost $= K_0\gamma$

Alternatively,

$K_0\gamma = M_0\ \bar{s}\ \bar{m}$ (both are expressions of first-period profits in excess of the cost of capital)

Where:

$M_0 \equiv initial\ market\ size$

$\bar{s} \equiv average\ market\ share$

$\bar{m} \equiv average\ profit\ margin\ above\ that\ needed\ to\ return\ the\ cost\ of\ capital$

Therefore, we can write:

$NPV = M_0\ g\ \bar{s}\ \bar{m}$ Which can be interpreted:

$NPV = Market\ Scale\ \cdot Power$

The derivation of the Fundamental Equation of Strategy thus used these simplifying assumptions:
1. n = n*
2. market growth is constant over n*
3. market share is constant over n*
4. differential returns are constant over n*
5. the business has a finite life

If one were to compare the value derived to actual market cap, in addition to altering these assumptions, one would have to add back the initial capital, account for price levels in the overall market, and add back excess assets on the balance sheet (accumulated cash for example).

13

PART I
STRATEGY STATICS

CHAPTER 1
SCALE ECONOMIES
SIZE MATTERS

Netflix Cracks the Code

This chapter begins our journey together to construct the 7 Powers. It and the six that follow will each cover one of the seven Power types. I start with Scale Economies and illustrate this Power with Netflix.

In the spring of 2003 I took a leap by investing in a small early-stage company based in Los Gatos, California. Today you may recognize the name: Netflix. Most of my investments have been in large caps, but I made this bet on Netflix due to their impressive mail-order DVD-rental business which was successfully disintermediating Blockbuster's brick-and-mortar business model. Blockbuster faced the unpleasant choice of losing market share or eliminating late fees, which accounted for about half of their income. The investment hypothesis was grounded in this dilemma: Blockbuster would drag their feet facing up to the painful existential imperatives that confronted them and Netflix would continue to cannibalize their customers.[14]

This hypothesis was borne out by Blockbuster's subsequent behavior and their eventual demise.

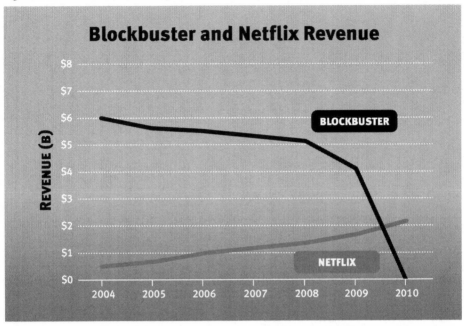

As discussed in my Introduction, a strategy must meet the high hurdle of "A route to continuing Power in a significant market." Netflix's DVD-by-mail business made the grade, and it was their Power over Blockbuster that sealed the deal.

But there was a long-term time fuse to this mail distribution business. Why? The physical DVD business would eventually be supplanted by digital streaming distribution. The timing was uncertain, but Moore's Law, coupled with the meteoric advances in Internet bandwidth and capability, guaranteed this outcome. The digital future was rising over the horizon, and Netflix could see it. There's a reason, after all, they hadn't dubbed their company Warehouse-Flix.

Streaming is a strategically separate business from DVDs by mail. By that I mean that the drivers of Power in each are largely orthogonal: different industry economics and different potential competitors. And streaming's Power prospects were not that encouraging: plummeting IT costs and rapid advances of cloud services suggested diminishing barriers. Anyone, it seemed, could set up a streaming business.

Netflix understood this but remained undaunted. First of all, they realized they had no choice but to embrace streaming; as astute strategists, they knew that if they didn't obsolete themselves, someone else would do it to them. And they were tactically smart. Given the uncertainty inherent in this emerging field, they took their time, demurring on high-testosterone bet-the-company antics. Instead, they modestly eased into streaming in 2007, hoping to test the waters and gain the needed experience. They accompanied this with much painstaking legwork, partnering with a dizzying array of electronic hardware streaming platform makers.

But deploying smart tactics, though complex and demanding, is not itself a strategy, and indeed any potential for Power remained opaque in those early days. For the time, Netflix could only stay alert and hope that Pasteur's dictum would eventually bear fruit and chance would favor their prepared minds.

For Netflix, the crucial insight didn't snap into focus until 2011, fully four years after they started streaming. Up till then, Netflix had negotiated with content owners (film studios being the chief example) for streaming rights. But these content owners were very savvy about monetizing their properties—they sliced and diced these rights by geographical region, release date, duration of the agreement, and so on. Ted Sarandos, Netflix's Chief Content Officer, came to believe that it was vital the company secure exclusive streaming rights to certain properties. Here now Netflix finally made a radical move: a major resource commitment to originals, starting with *House of Cards* in 2012.

On the face of it, Netflix's moves looked risky, overly ambitious. Creating originals, and thus tying up all the rights to that content, was more expensive. Further, Netflix had previously been down the road of original content with its Red Envelope Entertainment, and the results weren't pretty. So too did it seem now that such forward integration might prove "a bridge too far."

But these bold, counter-intuitive moves proved game-changing. Exclusive rights and originals made content, a major component of Netflix's cost structure, a fixed-cost item. Any potential streamer would now have to ante up the same number of dollars, regardless of how many subscribers they had. If, say, Netflix paid $100M for *House of Cards* and their streaming business had 30M customers, then the cost per customer was three dollars and change. In this scenario, a competitor with only one million subscribers would have to ante up $100 per subscriber. This was a radical change in industry economics, and it put to rest the specter of a value-destroying commodity rat race.[16]

Scale Economies—the First of the 7 Powers

The quality of declining unit costs with increased business size is referred to as Scale Economies. It is the first of the 7 Powers I will examine, and its conceptual lineage begins with Adam Smith's *Wealth of Nations* and indeed the beginnings of Economics itself.

Why do Scale Economies result in Power? Let's recall the conditions for Power laid out in the Introduction. Power is a configuration that creates the potential for persistent significant differential returns, even in the face of fully committed and competent competition. To fulfill this, two components must be simultaneously present:

1. A *Benefit*: some condition which yields material improvement in the cash flow of the Power wielder via reduced cost, enhanced pricing and/ or decreased investment requirements.

2. A *Barrier*: some obstacle which engenders in competitors an inability and/ or unwillingness to engage in behaviors that might, over time, arbitrage out this benefit.

For Scale Economies, the Benefit is straightforward: lowered costs. In the case of Netflix, their lead in subscribers translated directly in lower content costs *per subscriber* for originals and exclusives.

The Barrier, however, is subtler. What prevents other firms from competing this away? The answer lies in the likely interplay of well-managed competitors. Suppose a company has a significant scale advantage in a Scale Economies business. Smaller firms would spot this advantage, and their first impulse might be to pick up market share, thus improving their relative cost position and erasing some of this disadvantage while improving their bottom line. To get there, however, they would have to offer up better value to customers, such as lower prices.

In an established market, such tactics are visible to the leader, who would realize the threat of reducing their relative scale advantage; they would retaliate by using their superior cost position as a defensive redoubt (matching price cuts for example). After several bouts of this, a follower will come to expect such retaliation and build it into their financial models for the impact of gain-share moves. For them, such moves would inevitably destroy value, rather than create it.

Intel's microprocessor business that I discussed in the Introduction is a good example of how this plays out. Intel developed Scale Economies in the microprocessor business. Over a very long period, they were doggedly challenged by Advanced Micro Devices in this space. The outcome: a continuingly great business for Intel and persistent pain for AMD—at every turn Intel could fight off AMD relying on the economics rooted in its Scale Economies.

This unattractive cost/benefit is itself the Barrier for Scale Economies. Of course, it goes without saying: the Barrier must be thoughtfully maintained by the incumbent leader, but to bet on anything else would be foolish. So we see that Scale Economies satisfy the sufficient and necessary conditions for Power.

Scale Economies: *Benefit*: Reduced Cost

Barrier: Prohibitive Costs of Share Gains

This situation creates a very difficult position for Netflix's smaller-scale streaming competitors. If they offer the same deliverable as Netflix, similar amounts of content for the same price, their P&L will suffer. If they try to remediate this by offering less content or raising prices, customers will abandon their service and they will lose market share. Such a competitive cul-de-sac is the hallmark of Power.

The 7 Powers Chart

Scale Economies is only the first of seven Power types I will cover. To make it easier for you to track and compare them, let me now introduce the 7 Powers Chart. Chapter by chapter, as we move along, I will populate it with each additional Power type.

As noted above, Power requires a Benefit and a Barrier.

Figure 1.2

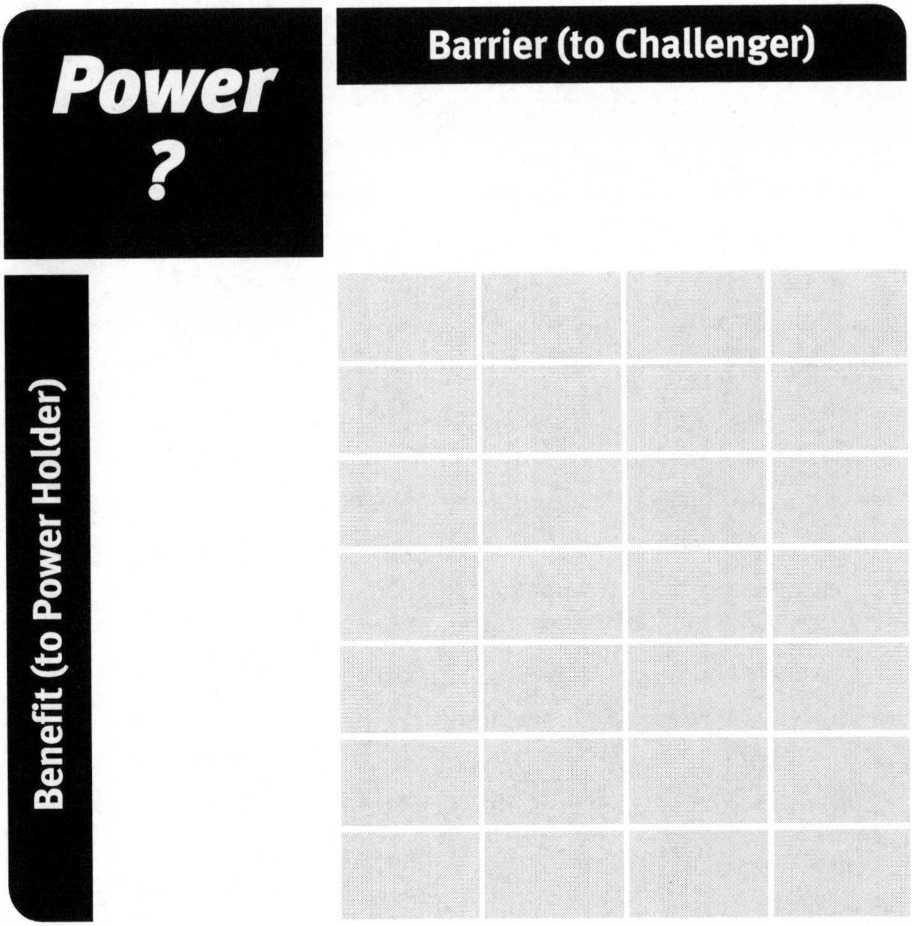

I can now build up the chart by providing granularity surrounding both the Benefit and the Barrier. With regard to the Benefit, cash flow is improved by (1) enhancing value (enabling higher pricing) and/or (2) lowering cost *ceteris paribus*.[17] With regard to the Barrier, a competitor fails to arbitrage out the Benefit because (1) they are unable to, or (2) they can, but refrain from so doing because they expect the outcome to be economically unattractive.

Figure 1.3

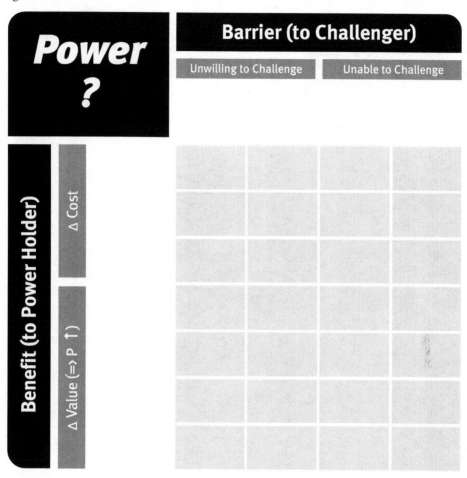

With this in hand, I can now populate the chart with our first Power type, Scale Economies:

Figure 1.4: Scale Economies in the 7 Powers

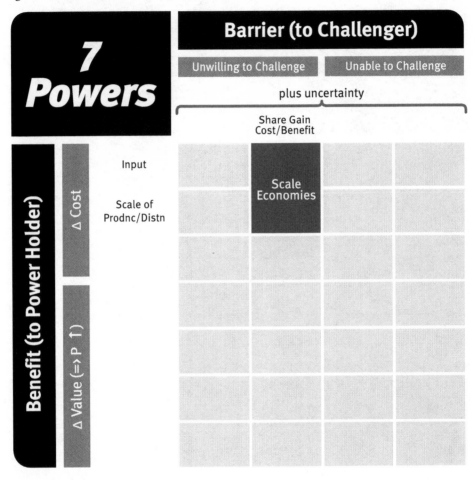

Here let's define Scale Economies:

> *A business in which per unit cost declines as production volume increases.*

In the Netflix example we see a feature of Scale Economies that recurs in many technology firms: a single fixed cost which declines per unit as it is prorated over higher and higher volumes.

Beyond fixed costs, Scale Economies emerge from other sources as well. To name a few:

- *Volume/area relationships.* These occur when production costs are closely tied to area, while their utility is tied to volume, resulting in lower per-volume costs with increasing scale. Bulk milk tanks and warehouses would serve as examples.

- *Distribution network density.* As the density of a distribution network increases to accommodate more customers per area, delivery costs decline as more economical route structures can be accommodated. A new entrant competitor to UPS would face this difficulty.

- *Learning economies.* If learning leads to a benefit (reduced cost or improved deliverables) and is positively correlated with production levels, then a scale advantage accrues to the leader.

- *Purchasing economies.* A larger scale buyer can often elicit better pricing for inputs. For example, this has helped Wal-Mart.

Value and Power

The sole objective of a strategy is to increase the potential value of the business. The chart below shows how Netflix fared after creating Power in their streaming business.

Netflix's share price trajectory is instructive. First, the payoff for their successful strategy was enormous. Over the above six years, Netflix's stock price increased six-fold compared to a doubling of the market. Second, we can observe that this outperformance was not monotonic—2010 to 2013 was a roller coaster, and later years were no walk in the park. Regarding this volatility:

- In situations of high flux, it often takes time for cash flow to reliably reflect Power, so investor expectations may move up and down.

- In our discussion of Power, I have been careful to characterize it as creating a *potential* for value, but this potential can only be realized when coupled with operational excellence. Netflix's plummet in 2011 was the result of

Figure 1.5: Netflix Stock Price vs. S&P 500 (8/2010 = 100%)[18]

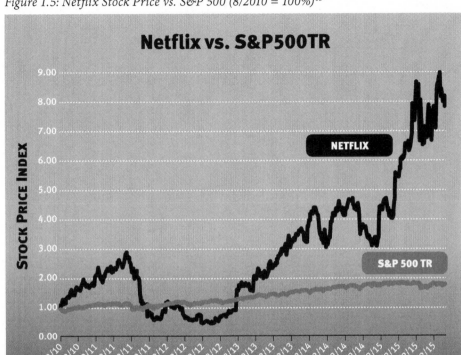

operational errors.[19] Though the period proved painful, their strategy still remained valid, and their Power intact, so these missteps were not fatal.

Parsing Power Intensity: Industry Economics + Competitive Position

Before leaving this chapter and moving on to the next type of Power, I would like to add a bit more structure to the characterization of Power itself.

Part of the tradecraft of economists consists of teasing out the essential nature of a problem by more formally modeling it. The art lies in selecting the simplifying assumptions: they must be chosen in a way that isolates the salient features of a problem, while not assuming away core characteristics.

As I noted earlier, the Barrier in Scale Economies comes from a follower's rational economic calculation (often learned) that, despite the attractive returns being earned by the leader, attack carries an unattractive payoff.

A productive way to more formally calibrate the intensity of the scale leader's Power is to assess the economic leeway they have in balancing attractive returns with appropriate retaliatory behavior to maintain share. The greater this leeway, the more attractive the longer-term equilibrium is likely to be for the leader.

To do this, let me introduce the notion of Surplus Leader Margin (SLM). This is the profit margin the business with Power can expect to achieve if pricing is such that its competitor's profits are zero. We derive the SLM for Netflix-like fixed cost Scale Economies in an Appendix to this chapter. If the fixed cost = C, then:

Surplus Leader Margin = [C/(Leader Sales)] * [(Leader Sales)/(Follower Sales) – 1][20]

The first term of this equation indicates the relative significance of fixed cost in the company's overall financials, while the second term shows the degree of scale advantage. Put another way:

Surplus Leader Margin = [Scale Economy Intensity] * [Scale Advantage]

Namely, the first term is tied to the economic structure of that industry (the intensity of the scale economy), a condition faced by all firms. The second term reflects the position of the leader relative to the follower. For Power to exist, both of these terms must be significantly positive. For example, even if there exists strong potential scale economies (C is large, relative to sales), the leader margin will still be zero (no Power) without any scale differential, because that second term was still zero, too.

This parsing of Power intensity into the separate strata of industry economics and competitive position is critical for a practitioner as it applies to most types of Power. In any assessment of Power, both need to be understood independently, and both are fair game for strategy initiatives.[21] Here, with their streaming business, Netflix launched a two-pronged assault. Their thrust into exclusives and originals changed the economic structure of the industry, while their early-in and thoughtful rollout gave them a scale advantage. If Netflix had accepted the existing industry economic structure as an unalterable given, then no route to Power would have been available in streaming, and their value prospects would have remained quite dim, dependent on a declining DVD rental business.

So as we discuss each type of Power in the coming chapters, in addition to the 7 Powers Chart, I will roll up another table summarizing the nature of these two dimensions, which together govern the intensity of Power. Here is our first addition:

Figure 1.6: Power Intensity Determinants

	Industry Economics	*Competitive Position*
Scale Economies	Scale economy intensity	Relative scale

Scale Economies: Summing Up

Netflix's streaming business is the driver of its remarkable rise to its double-digit billion market capitalization. Getting there has required the relentless pursuit of excellence in every corner of the company. Such dedication and focus is essential for creating value, but it is not sufficient. In addition, Netflix's success could only emerge once they had crafted a route to continuing Power in significant markets—in other words, a strategy. The cornerstone of this strategy was moving to exclusives and originals which enabled them to wield their scale as a source of profound leverage. Such Scale Economies fully satisfy our definition of Power: the Benefit flowing from the reduction in content cost enabled by their vast pool of subscribers, and the Barrier resulting from the unattractive cost/benefit of market share onslaughts.

Appendix 1.1: Derivation of Surplus Leader Margin for Scale Economies

To calibrate the intensity of Power, I ask the question "What governs profitability of the company with Power (S) when prices are such that the company with no Power (W) makes no profit at all?"

This Appendix explores Scale Economies from a fixed cost. There are sources of Scale Economies other than a fixed cost but this is a common one.

Total cost $= c\,Q + C$

Where $c \equiv$ variable cost per unit

$Q \equiv$ units produced

$C \equiv$ fixed cost (during each production period as opposed to start-up)

$\therefore$ Profits $(\pi) = (P - c)\,Q - C$

Where $P \equiv$ price faced by all sellers

There are two businesses: S, the strong company, and W, the weak company

As an indication of leader leverage, assess:

Surplus Leader Margin: What governs S's margins if P is set $\ni {}_W\pi = 0$?

$_W\pi = 0 \Rightarrow \qquad 0 = (P - c)\,_WQ - C$

$\qquad\qquad$ Or $\qquad P = c + C/_WQ$

$_S\pi \qquad = (P - c)\,_SQ - C$

Substituting in formula for P

$= ([c + C/_WQ] - c)\,_SQ - C$

$= [C/_WQ]_SQ - C$

$= C\,(_SQ - {}_WQ)/_WQ$

OR

S' margin $\equiv {}_S\pi/_S$Revenue $= {}_S\pi/(P\,_SQ) = [C/(P\,_SQ)][\,(_SQ - {}_WQ)/\,_WQ\,]$

$$\boxed{\textbf{Surplus Leader Margin} = [C/(P\,_SQ)]\,[_SQ/_WQ{-}1]}$$

$[_SQ/\,_WQ - 1]$: Competitive Position—relative market share beyond parity

$[C/(P\,_SQ)]$: Industry Economics—the relative importance of the fixed cost

CHAPTER 2
NETWORK ECONOMIES
GROUP VALUE

BranchOut Takes on LinkedIn

In June of 2010 Rick Marini had a problem. He needed to track down a contact at a particular company—he was certain he knew someone there but just couldn't recall the name. To most people this would constitute a soon forgotten frustration. But Marini was not most people. He was a Harvard Business School trained serial entrepreneur with significant recruiting industry experience—he had founded both SuperFan and Tickle.com, selling the latter to Monster Worldwide for nearly $100M.

So a month later he launched BranchOut, a professional networking Facebook app. Marini went at this hard and by September had pulled together a $6M Series A round led by Accel Partners, Floodgate and Norwest Venture Partners with some notable tech firm execs joining the round as well.

Recruiters want to make the best use of their time, so they go to the source with the largest number of listed professionals, while at the same time professionals want to list their names on the site with the most recruiters visiting. Such one-hand-shakes-the-other self-reinforcing upward spirals are known as Network Economies[22]:

the value of the service to each customer is enhanced as new customers join the "network." In such a situation, having the most customers is everything, and Marini knew exactly how this game was played: rapidly scale or die.

Catch-up is usually impossible if there are Network Economies and LinkedIn already had 70M members. But Marini was betting that the game was not yet over. His idea was to build on Facebook's base, which was almost 10x that of LinkedIn, enabling this with tools so that a user could seamlessly download all their information from LinkedIn. Marini positioned a Facebook tie-in as a key to better value:

> "Facebook has a strength of connection that LinkedIn doesn't have. LinkedIn is someone you met at a conference. Facebook is your true support network."

Marini's tactics seemed to get a lot of traction: users ballooned in Q1 2011 from 10,000 to 500,000. Armed with this hyper-scaling, Marini raised an $18M Series B round in May of 2011.

It did not stop there. The company received numerous awards including selection amongst the FASTech50 for 2011. Monthly active users accelerated and investors poured in more money, bringing total investment to $49 million. LinkedIn's wildly successful IPO on May 19, 2011, with the share price doubling in a day, seemed further confirmation that the space was hot.

Users continued to grow rapidly, peaking around 14 million in the spring of 2012. But then, as the graph below details, the party ended and the numbers fell off a cliff. *TechCrunch* explained the collapse this way:

> Few of BranchOut's users were truly engaged, and the recruitment search tool it planned to make money with never got serious traction. When Facebook banned the spammy wall post method, BranchOut's churn quickly outpaced its growth and the company deflated. The train tracks were stripped out from under it.

In September of 2014 Hearst acquired the assets and team of BranchOut, ending the company.

Figure 2.1: BranchOut Monthly Active Users (millions, January 1, 2012–June 23, 2012)[23]

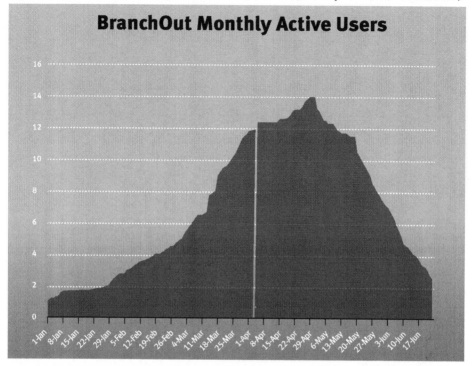

The success of all three parties on this dance card, BranchOut, Facebook and LinkedIn, was predicated on users' value of the service depending on the presence of others, the central feature of Network Economies. Their founders were fully aware of this business characteristic and aggressively and competently pushed tactics fully consistent with this understanding. Facebook and LinkedIn could co-exist because their respective networks were walled off from one another: users wanted to keep their personal lives (Facebook) separate from their work lives (LinkedIn). BranchOut hoped to build a bridge between the two, but it just didn't fly. Users wanted this wall maintained, a lesson Facebook themselves learned in their failed rollout of Facebook at Work.

Network Economies can result in high Power intensity and some great businesses are built on them: IBM mainframes, operating systems for Microsoft, Steinway Pianos and Exchange Traded Funds.

The Benefit and the Barrier

Network Economies occur when the value of a product to a customer is increased by the use of the product by others. Returning to our Benefit/Barrier characterization of Power:

- *Benefit.* A company in a leadership position with Network Economies can charge higher prices than its competitors, because of the higher value as a result of more users. For example, the value of LinkedIn's HR Solutions Suite comes from the numbers of LinkedIn users, so LinkedIn can charge more than a competing product with fewer participants.

- *Barrier.* The barrier for Network Economies is the unattractive cost/benefit of gaining share, and this can be extremely high. In particular the value deficit of a follower can be so large that the price discount needed to offset this is unthinkable. For example, "What would BranchOut have had to offer users for them to use BranchOut rather than LinkedIn?" I think most observers would agree that every user would have required a non-trivial payment, so the total spend for BranchOut would have been colossal.

Industries exhibiting Network Economies often exhibit these attributes:

- *Winner take all.* Businesses with strong Network Economies are frequently characterized by a tipping point: once a single firm achieves a certain degree of leadership, then the other firms just throw in the towel. Game over—the P&L of a challenge would just be too ugly. For example, even a company as competent and with as deep pockets as Google could not unseat Facebook with Google+.

- *Boundedness.* As powerful as this Barrier is, it is bounded by the character of the network, something well-demonstrated by the continued success of both Facebook and LinkedIn. Facebook has powerful Network Economies itself but these have to do with personal not professional interactions. The boundaries of the network effects determine the boundaries of the business.

- *Decisive early product.* Due to tipping point dynamics, early relative scaling is critical in developing Power. Who scales the fastest is often determined by who gets the product most right early on. Facebook's trumping of MySpace is a good example.

This Benefit/Barrier combination allows me to place Network Economies on the 7 Powers Chart.

Figure 2.2: Network Economies in the 7 Powers

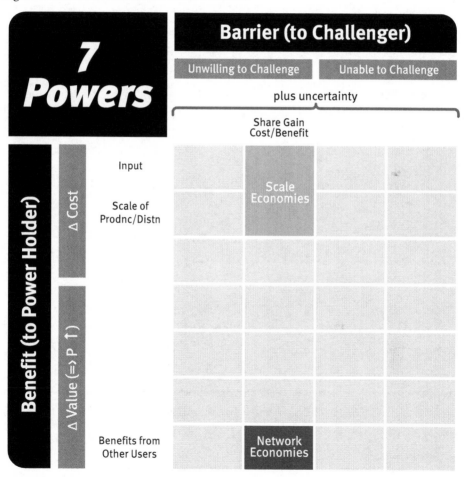

Network Economies definition:

A business in which the value realized by a customer increases as the installed base increases.

Network Economies: Industry Economics and Competitive Position

Power insures the ability to earn outsized returns well into the future, driving up value. This is captured by the Benefit/Barrier requirement. As before in Chapter 1, I will use Surplus Leader Margin to calibrate the intensity of Power: "What governs the leader's profitability when prices are such that the challenger makes no profit at all?"

In the case of Network Economies, I assume all costs are variable (c), so the challenger's profit is zero when the price equals these variable costs. The value the leader offers is greater than this by the differential network benefits it offers, and I assume they can bump up price to account for this.

$$\text{Surplus Leader Margin}[24] = 1 - 1/[1+\delta(_sN - _wN)]$$

Where δ = the benefit which accrues to each existing network member when one more member joins the network divided by the variable cost per unit of production

$_sN$ = the installed base of the leader

$_wN$ = the installed base of the follower

δ is a measure of the intensity of Network Economies: how important the network effect is relative to industry costs. This formula is of course stylized. In a real world situation like that faced by BranchOut, LinkedIn and Facebook, the value of the benefit of others on the network is more complex. For example, it would not be expected to be strictly linear: if you are a US college student on Facebook, another user in Ulan Bator is likely to be of far less value to you than the presence of one of your classmates.

It was the hope of Marini and his investors that the δ of BranchOut would be driven by the absolute installed base leadership of Facebook rather than keyed to the more narrowly defined "professional" space installed base of BranchOut. It turned out that there was very little spillover. This meant that LinkedIn had an insurmountable advantage in this space.

$[_sN - _wN]$ is the leader's absolute advantage in installed base. As you would expect, as this approaches zero, the Surplus Leader Margin also approaches zero, even if the industry has strong Network Economies. This equation also makes evident the tipping point outcome of Network Economies. As the installed base difference gets large, the pricing such that the follower has zero profits results in very large leader margins (100% at the limit). This means a leader can price at very attractive margins while still pricing well below the breakeven point for the follower. The result is that a follower would have to price at a significant loss to offer equivalent value. As pointed out earlier, in BranchOut's case it would not surprise me if users would have had to be paid (a negative price) to switch from LinkedIn.

So once again I have parsed the intensity of a Power type into separate components: one reflecting industry economics (δ, the degree to which network economies exist in a particular business) and the other competitive position ($[_sN - _wN]$) within that structure. As noted in the last chapter, these need to be understood independently.

Figure 2.3: Power Intensity Determinants

	Industry Economics	**Competitive Position**
Scale Economies	Scale economy intensity	Relative scale
Network Economies	Intensity of network effect	Absolute difference in installed base

Appendix 2.1: Derivation of Surplus Leader Margin for Network Economies

To calibrate the intensity of Power, I ask the question "What governs profitability of the company with Power (S) when prices are such that the company with no Power (W) makes no profit at all?"

The total network size (#users) $\equiv N = {_s}N + {_w}N$

Where S is the strong company and W the weak company

Suppose for simplicity the network effects are homogeneous; then S is able to charge a price premium:

$${_s}P - {_w}P = \delta [{_s}N - {_w}N] \text{ where } \delta \equiv \text{ the marginal benefit to all users from one joiner}$$

There are no scale economies so

Profit in a time period $\equiv \pi = [P - c] Q$

with $P \equiv$ price

        $c \equiv$ variable cost per unit

        $Q \equiv$ units produced per time period

As an indication of leverage, assess:

What governs S's margins if P is set $\ni {_w}\pi = 0$?

$_w\pi = 0 \Rightarrow$ $0 = (P - c) {_w}Q$ $\Rightarrow {_w}P = c$

S can charge a premium so, ${_s}P = \delta [{_s}N - {_w}N] + c$

$\therefore$ ${_s}\pi = [(\delta [{_s}N - {_w}N] + c) - c] {_s}Q$

        ${_s}\pi = [\delta ({_s}N - {_w}N)] {_s}Q$

Surplus Leader Margin $\equiv {_s}$Margin $= [\delta ({_s}N - {_w}N)]/[(\delta [{_s}N - {_w}N] + c)]$

${_s}$Margin $= \delta [{_s}N - {_w}N]/[(\delta [{_s}N - {_w}N] + 1]]$

Surplus Leader Margin $= 1 - 1/[(\delta/c) ({_s}N - {_w}N) + 1]$

Competitive Position: $[{_s}N - {_w}N]$—Absolute difference in installed base

Industry Economics: δ/c—The value increases with each additional user per dollar variable cost

If ${_s}N = {_w}N$, then SLM = 0; as ${_s}N \gg {_w}N$, SLM $\to$ 100% with $\delta > 0$

Some comments on Network Economies:

- There can be positive network effects but no potential for Power.
  - The network effect δ needs to be large enough relative to the potential installed base and the cost structure for there even to be one profitable player as this fulfills the Benefit condition. If homogeneous network effects are the only value source, then if N δ < c, a firm cannot reach profitability.

  - This is the problem I see often in Silicon Valley. If one supposes Network Economies then the strategy imperative is to scale much faster than anyone else—if another firm gets to the tipping point before you, then the game is over.

  - However, *ex ante* it is often very difficult to have much assurance in sizing potential N and δ. So you are left with a situation that sometimes requires significant up front capital but an uncertain ability to monetize. This for example has plagued Twitter. Usually management gets the blame but we are back to Buffett's observation: "When a manager with a reputation for brilliance tackles a business with a reputation for bad economics, the reputation of the business remains intact."[25]

- Network effects can be very complex. As indicated earlier, however, there are many excellent treatments so I have been brief. A common twist I have not covered are indirect network effects (also called demand side network effects).
  - If a business has important complements and these complements are somehow exclusive to each offering, then a leader will attract more and/or better complements.

  - As a result the entire value proposition to a customer is improved (increasing SLM for example).

  - An example of this would be smartphone apps. Another smartphone OS would be hard to offer at this point because it would start out with a dearth of apps. This would make it very unattractive. Developers of apps would of course not be incented to spend their scarce resources since the market would be small.

○ Note that in this case the contribution of additional complements is not linear.

CHAPTER 3
COUNTER-POSITIONING
SCYLLA AND CHARYBDIS

Bogle's Folly

This chapter introduces Counter-Positioning, the next Power type. I developed this concept to depict a not well-understood competitive dynamic I often have observed both as a strategy advisor and an equity investor. I must confess it is my favorite form of Power, both because of my authorship and because it is so contrarian. As we will see, it is an avenue for defeating an incumbent who appears unassailable by conventional wisdom metrics of competitive strength.

The case that I start out with is just such a contest, Vanguard's assault on the world of active equity management. Everyone now knows Vanguard as the poster child for low-cost passive index funds by which they have become one of the largest asset managers in the world. But their founder, John C. Bogle, faced a very different world at the inception of Vanguard, a world in which active equity management ruled the day. So, to our story.

On May 1, 1975, John C. Bogle carried the day by persuading the reluctant Wellington Management board to back Vanguard. Vanguard's charter was radical: the new investment management company would initiate an equity mutual fund that simply tracked the market, dispensing with any pretensions of active management. Not only that, but it would also operate "at cost"—owned by the funds it administered, paying all returns back to shareholders. The following year, the third innovation was put in place: Vanguard became a no-load fund—one with no sales commissions.

Creating something really new in business is challenging in the best of times. Vanguard was no exception; its gestation period was attenuated and its birth painful. Bogle traces its roots as far back as his Princeton senior thesis, penned twenty-five years before, in 1950. In 1969, when Wells Fargo began pioneering index funds, Bogle took note. He also drew inspiration from foundational academic work, in particular Paul Samuelson's seminal 1974 piece for *The Journal of Portfolio Management*, in which the Nobel Laureate in Economics envisioned a fund that would enable investors to simply track the market.

Bogle attracted prominent underwriters, and the fund launched in August of 1976. You could charitably describe the reception as unenthusiastic: only $11M trickled in from investors. Soon after the launch, Samuelson himself lauded the effort in his column for *Newsweek*, but with little result: the fund had reached only $17M by mid-1977. Vanguard's operating model depended on others for distribution, and brokers in particular were put off by a product that was predicated on the notion that they provided no value in helping their clients choose which active funds to select.

Swimming against the riptide of self-interest in the investment business is not for the faint of heart, but Bogle's bull terrier grip on his new business model was implacable, and he vigorously enjoined the battle. Of course, Vanguard, by design, possessed a fundamental advantage in the iron law of active management: the average gross return of active funds has to equal the market return, and since their expenses are substantially higher than passive funds, their average net returns will always be less than those of passive funds. Complementing this is the lack of significant serial correlation of returns in active funds' ability to best the market—this year's winner has little advantage for next year. Inevitably the outcome of this is that active funds are on average a loser's game as indicated by the chart below.

Vanguard's inauspicious starting capital was followed by modest growth in assets. A merger with Exeter helped, and bit by bit the company achieved respectable scale, as the chart below indicates. Still, more than a decade would

pass before Vanguard reached full escape velocity. Once it did take off, however, the upward arc was stunning with assets under management exceeding $3T by the end of 2015.

Figure 3.2: Vanguard Assets Under Management (1975–2015)[27]:

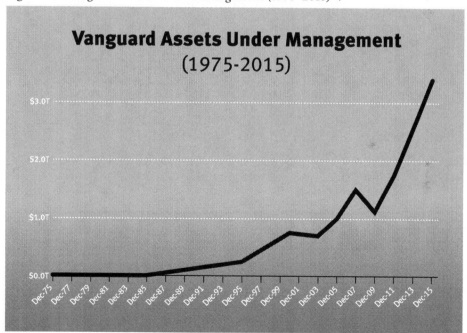

Fueling the fire, too, was the advent of exchange-traded funds (ETFs), which more often than not mimicked the low cost and passive approach pioneered by Vanguard. What had started as a trickle now became a torrent: as the chart below indicates, in the 7 years from 2007 to 2013, actively managed mutual funds gave up $600B while ETFs and domestic equity mutual funds gained more than $700B.

Figure 3.3: Cumulative Investment Flows by Fund Type[28]

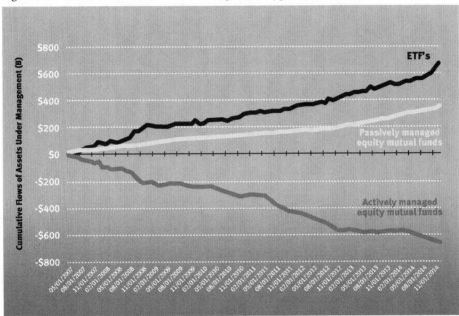

Counter-Positioning: the Benefit and Barrier

There are few occurences in business as complex as the emergence and eventual success of a new business model. Think of the diverse circumstances attending Vanguard's rise: huge and successful incumbent active mutual funds, a committed entrepreneur, an advancing intellectual frontier, fast-improving computer technology, entrenched channel disincentives, consumer misinformation, and so on.

In situations like this, it falls to the strategist to carefully peel back the layers of complexity and eventually seize upon some irreduceable kernel of insight amidst the competitive reality.

To understand the ascendancy of Vanguard, I must first note these characteristics:

1. An upstart who developed a superior, heterodox business model.
2. That business model's ability to successfully challenge well-entrenched and formidable incumbents.
3. The steady accumulation of customers, all while the incumbent remains seemingly paralyzed and unable to respond.

These elements were not unique to Vanguard—they were pieces of an oft-repeated story. Think of Dell vs. Compaq, Nokia vs. Apple, Amazon vs. Borders, In-N-Out vs. McDonalds, Charles Schwab vs. Merrill Lynch, Netflix vs. Blockbuster, etc. But nearly always, these featured the same outcome: the incumbent responds either not at all or too late.

These victories aren't born of happenstance, of course; they are strategic, and the upstarts usually succeed in creating a lot of value for themselves, while severely diminishing that of the incumbents.

Returning to our Benefit/Barrier characterization of Power:

- *Benefit.* The new business model is superior to the incumbent's model due to lower costs and/or the ability to charge higher prices. In Vanguard's case, their business model resulted in substantially lower costs (the elimination of expensive portfolio managers, as well as the reduction of channel costs and unnecessary trading costs) which then translated into superior product deliverables (higher average net returns). Due to their business structure of returning profits to their fund-holders, they realized value from market share gains ($\bar{s}$ in the fundamental equation of strategy), rather than ramping up differential profit margins ($\bar{m}$).

- *Barrier.* The barrier for Counter-Positioning seems a bit mysterious: how could a powerhouse (such as Fidelity Investments in this case) allow itself to be persistently humbled by an upstart over such an extended period? Couldn't they foresee the potential success of Vanguard's model? Freqently in such situations, naïve onlookers castigate the incumbent for lack of vision, or even just poor management. Often, too, they level this accusation at companies with prior plaudits for business acumen. In many cases, this view is unjust and misleading. The incumbent's failure to respond, more often than not, results from thoughtful calculation. They observe the upstart's new model, and ask, "Am I better off staying the course, or adopting the new model?" Counter-Positioning applies to the subset of cases in which the expected damage to the existing business elicits a "no" answer from the incumbent. The Barrier, simply put, is collateral damage. In the Vanguard case, Fidelity looked at their highly attractive active management franchise and concluded that the new passive funds' more modest returns would likely fail to offset the damage done by a migration from their flagship products.

With this preliminary understanding, I can now place Counter-Positioning on the 7 Powers Chart:

Figure 3.4: Counter-Positioning in the 7 Powers

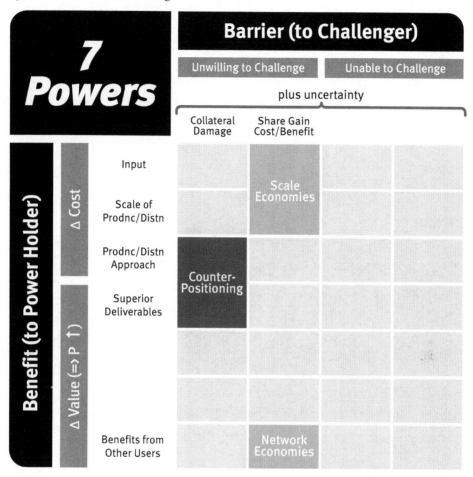

This allows me to define Counter-Positioning:

> *A newcomer adopts a new, superior business model which the incumbent does not mimic due to anticipated damage to their existing business.*

The Varieties of Collateral Damage

There can be several possible reasons for the incumbent's failure to mimic the upstart. In this section I will detail those differences, as knowing them will clarify the correct strategic posture. Here's a useful way to visualize this: imagine the incumbent CEO's business development team must evaluate the prudence of investing in the challenger's new approach.

Stand-Alone Unattractive is Not Counter-Positioning. In its first step, the business development team would hive off those situations in which a stand-alone assessment of the new approach forecasts an unattractive return, as these are not Counter-Positioning. To this end, the team would pose this question:

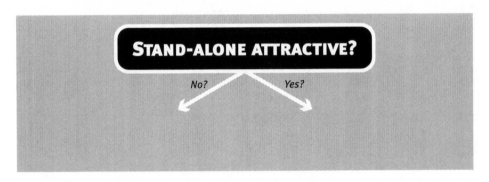

If "No" is the answer, then collateral damage does not account for the incumbent's rejection of the challenger's approach to the business. The new approach is simply a poor bet all by itself.

Here the example of the digital camera challenge to Kodak is instructive. Kodak's business model was legendary, built on the customer's continuing need to purchase film, a product in which Kodak was wildly profitable due to both Scale Economies and a proprietary edge (this Power type is Cornered Resources, to be covered in Chapter 6). Kodak offered the first of its path-breaking Brownie cameras in 1900. By 1930 it was one of the firms in the Dow Jones Industrial index, and it stayed in that group for more than 40 years—one of the great business empires.

Until digital photography came along, that is. Anyone could extrapolate from Moore's Law that analog chemical film was eventually doomed. Pundits have looked back and chided Kodak for poor management, lack of vision, and organizational inertia, and a reasonable person might well ask, "How could a company high on the lists of the best companies in the world succumb to such a defeat?"

A reasonable question. And the answer is much simpler than many suggest: in fact, Kodak was fully aware of its eventual fate and spent lavishly to explore survival options, but digital photography simply was not an attractive business opportunity for the company. Kodak's business model was built on its Power in film—it was not a camera company. The digital substitute for film was semiconductor storage, and Kodak brought nothing to this arena. As a company, Kodak had excellent management; thus the observed wheel-spinning, their fruitless explorations in the digital world, simply reflected the strategic cul-de-sac they faced. The technological frontier had moved: consumers were better off, but Kodak was not.

More generally this situation can be characterized by three conditions:

1. A new superior approach is developed (lower costs and/or improved features).
2. The products from the new approach exhibit a high degree of substitutability for the products from the old approach. In this case, as semiconductor topologies shrunk, digital imaging came to completely supplant chemical imaging.
3. The incumbent has little prospect for Power in this new business: either the industry economics support no Power (a commodity), or the incumbent's competitive position is such that attainment of Power is unlikely. Kodak's formidable strengths had little relevance to semiconductor memory, and those new products were on an inevitable path to commodization.

Such reinvention is quite common, as are the associated, and often unfair, castigations of the incumbent's management failures. "The gales of destruction" was Schumpeter's famous turn of phrase for such occurrences.

But this is not Counter-Positioning. Kodak's failure to respond had nothing to do with collateral damage within their film business; rather it indicated only that digital photography as a stand-alone business failed to offer even the faintest promise of Power for Kodak.

Facing such a situation, our hypothetical CEO would nix any commitment of investment, branching in the following way:

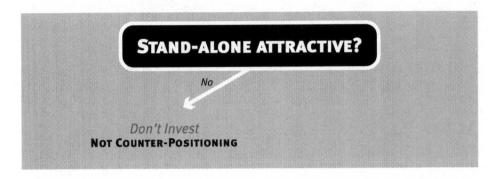

Before turning to those cases in which collateral damage serves as the decisive inhibitor, I would like to comment on another frequently discussed issue. Kodak could have easily taken the view that their business was image storage, not film, thus avoiding "marketing myopia."[29] Unfortunately this broader view of the business would have been to no avail, as the lack of semi-conductor capabilties would have remained and been decisive in determining a negative outcome.

1. **Milking: Negative Combined NPV.** Suppose the new approach was unlike digital storage for Kodak and instead looked promising on a stand-alone basis. In this case, our hypothetical CEO would face another set of issues:

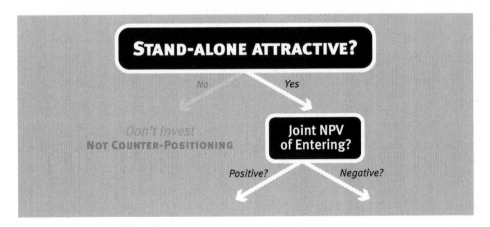

This was the situation faced by Ned Johnson, the CEO of Fidelity, when passive mutual funds started to appear. Unlike the Kodak case, Fidelity possessed all the capabilities to develop and distribute passive funds. They were a mutual fund powerhouse, and one could even reasonably argue that their capabilities in this space were superior to those of challenger Vanguard.

However, the impact of entry into passive funds on their remaining base business of active funds would have been subtractive. Active funds carry radically higher expense charges and many even had upfront sales commissions (loads). For the assets they would have cannibalized, the revenue decline would have been dramatic. Further, many at Fidelity felt they were facing an existential threat, and the introduction of passive funds would have taken them off-message in the rearguard advocacy of active funds. They assumed, reasonably, that any conceivable gains made with these new funds would have been more than offset by losses in their base business of active funds.

In similar hypotheticals, then, a rational incumbent CEO would decide to eschew the new approach. This type of "don't invest" determination represents one type of Counter-Positioning (CP). The term I use is "Milk" because the CEO is essentially choosing to milk a declining original business even though the new model is attractive.

To be explicit, while the decision to invest may have offset damage to the incumbent's original business (collateral damage), there remain some advantages to the decision to kill that investment. This is the Barrier.

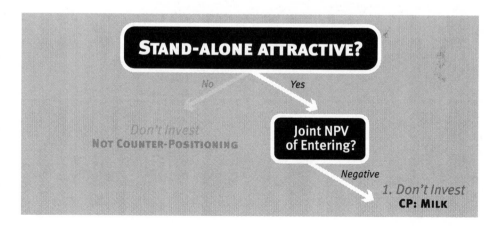

There is a dynamic to CP: Milk has practical importance, especially for the challenger. As the challenger cannibalizes the incumbent's customer base, two parts of the incumbent's negative attribution lessen: (a) the incumbent's original business shrinks, and (b) the uncertainty surrounding the viability of the challenger's approach diminishes. As this scenario plays out, the risk-adjusted size of expected collateral damage declines. At some point, a rational incumbent, our hypothetical CEO, will then find the collateral damage insufficiently off-setting—an investment is warranted. Such delayed entry happens frequently, and while some may characterize it as incumbent foot-dragging, it is often simply a rational response to the circumstances.

2. **History's Slave: Cognitive Bias.** Suppose an outside objective analyst examined the incumbent's potential entry into the challenger's new business model and found that the incremental NPV of doing so was positive. Certainly this would warrant an investment, yes? Not so fast. There's more to our collateral damage story. Thoughtful CEOs still might forego entry investment if their opinions differed from this objective view and they perceived deeper decrements.

Our next effort, then, is to explore reasons for such a difference:

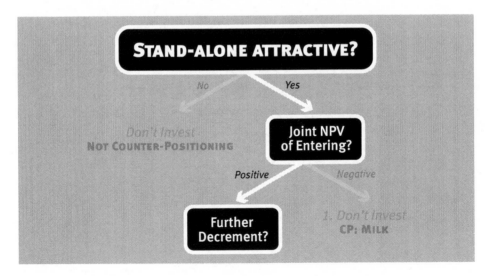

What are the potential causes of such decrements? They could be numerous, but over several decades of client strategy work, I have noted two that seem common. The first involves two characterisitics of challenges to incumbency:

1. The challenger's approach is novel and, at first, unproven. As a consquence, it is shrouded in uncertainty, especially to those looking in from the outside. The low signal-to-noise of the situation only heightens that uncertainty.

2. The incumbent has a successful business model. This heritage is influential and deeply embedded, as suggested by Nelson and Winter's[30] notion of "routines," and with it comes a certain view of how the world works. The CEO probably can't help but view circumstances through this lens, at least in part.

Together these two characteristics frequently lead incumbents to at first belittle the new approach, grossly underestimating its potential. In the face of low-cost passive funds, Ned Johnson of Fidelity once famously inquired, "Why would anyone settle for average returns?" This negative cognitive bias can lead to a "don't invest" decision, even if an objective observer might judge such an investment favorably. Here we arrive to the second type of Counter-Positioning:

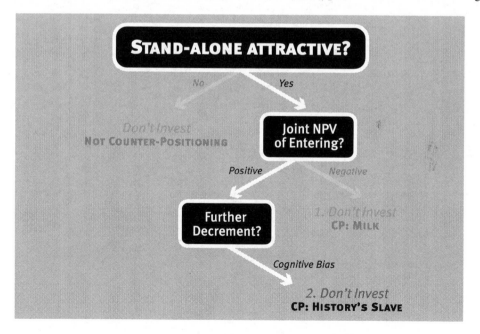

3. **Job Security: Agency Issues.** There's a second source of decrement that can lead our CEO to reject an objectively attractive investment decision: the differences between the objective of the firm (maximum value) and that of the CEO, or other investment decision-makers. Economists refer to these situations as "agency problems" because the agent's actions are at odds with the organization she represents.

Usually, it's about incentives. For example, it is devilishly difficult to design a CEO's compensation so that it closely mimics long-term enterprise value. Addressing the threat of a Counter-Positioned competitor frequently requires upending the incumbent's business in multiple ways, and such turmoil is rarely symmetric in its impact on enterprise value and compensation, even with best practice Long-Term Incentive Plans in place.

This completes our parsing of the collateral damage Barrier in Counter-Positioning:

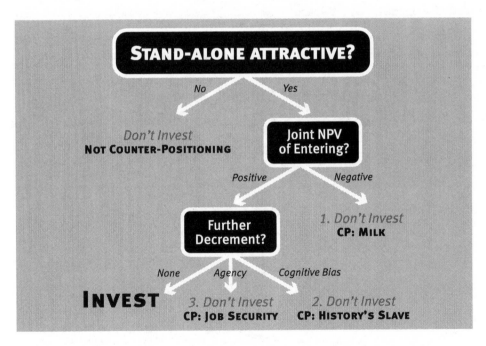

As the finalized chart indicates, there are three varieties of Counter-Positioning, depending on the particulars of the collateral damage involved: Milk, History's Slave and Job Security. I should note that Agency and Cognitive Bias issues are not mutually exclusive; frequently they appear in concert, as they are connected with the to-and-fro that accompanies the upending of a well-established business.

To finish up our treatment of Counter-Positioning, I will cover three more topics in this chapter: the relationship of Counter-Positioning to the well-known concept of Disruptive Technologies, some general comments about the characteristics of Counter-Positioning and finally some simple illustrative math.

Counter-Positioning versus Disruptive Technologies

I have benefited from the scholarship of Clayton Christensen and from his deep insight into the currents of technical change. His work is so well-known in the business world that I felt obliged to map my view of Counter-Positioning to his notion of Disruptive Technologies.

At the heart of Counter-Positioning lies the development of a new business model that, over time, has the potential to supplant the old. In the more general sense of the word, it is disruptive. However, when we consider the more specific meaning of Disruptive Technologies (DT) developed by Christensen, the waters muddy. Consider these examples:

- Kodak vs. digital photography. This is a DT, but not CP.

- In-N-Out vs. McDonald's. This is CP, but not DT (no new technology involved).

- Netflix streaming vs. HBO via cable. This is both CP and DT.

As evinced by the list, the concepts are not at all synonymous. Or more formally, there is a many-to-many mapping. This is also true more generally: there is a many-to-many mapping of all Power Types to Disruptive Technologies. Because Disruptive Technologies tell us nothing about Power they do not inform us about value.[31] Because of this, the subject is only a sidebar in the Statics of Strategy.

With the Dynamics of Strategy, a topic developed later in this book, Christensen's work has far more bearing. In Part II, we will learn that invention is the first cause of Power. It does not necessarily lead to Power, but it can sometimes create the circumstances in which Power may be established. Disruption, of course, is one consequence of invention.

Observations on Counter-Positioning

Before wrapping up this chapter, I want to offer up a few observations about Counter-Positioning that will be specifically useful to a strategist.

- As noted in the Introduction, Power must be considered relative to each competitor, actual and implicit. With Counter-Positioning, this is particulary important, because this type of Power only applies relative to the incumbent and says nothing regarding Power relative to other firms utilizing the new business model. So it remains only a partial strategy. To assure value creation, it must be complemented by a route to Power respective to other like competitors. For example, In-N-Out has Counter-Positioning Power over McDonald's, but this helps them not at all in facing like competitors such as Five Guys Burgers and Fries.

- As noted in our discussion of the collateral damage types, Cognitive Bias can play a role in deterring the incumbent. But the challenger, by its posture, may be able to influence such a move. How to attempt this? In its ascendancy, the challenger should avoid the temptation of trumpeting its superiority, instead suppressing that urge and adopting a tone of respect toward the incumbent. This behavior may result in the incumbent delaying objective cognition, giving the challenger a headstart on the new business model.

- Counter-Positioning is not an exclusive source of Power. The two prior chapters covered Power types that were exclusive: there could be only one company with Power. This is a reflection of the "Competitor Position" portion of the leverage calculation I have detailed. For these earlier types, there can be only one firm with a favorable competitive position. In contrast, there could be—and often are, in fact—many challengers Counter-Positioned respective to the incumbent.

- A Counter-Positioning challenge is one of the toughest management challenges. When I started teaching at Stanford in 2008, Nokia was the leader in smartphones. By 2014 they had disappeared from this market. Their CEO Stephen Elop's "Burning Platform" memo in 2011 captures well the immense frustration of a Counter-Positoned incumbent:

> *While competitors poured flames on our market share, what happened at Nokia? We fell behind, we missed big trends, and we lost time. At that time, we thought we were making the right decisions; but, with the benefit of hindsight, we now find ourselves years behind.*
>
> *The first iPhone shipped in 2007, and we still don't have a product that is close to their experience. Android came on the scene just over 2 years ago, and this week they took our leadership position in smartphone volumes. Unbelievable.*
>
> — *Stephen Elop, Nokia CEO*

- Though this isn't always the case, I have noticed a frequently repeated script for how an incumbent reacts to a CP challenge. I whimsically refer to it as the Five Stages of Counter-Positioning:

  1. Denial
  2. Ridicule
  3. Fear
  4. Anger
  5. Capitulation (frequently too late)

Elop's comments above reflect the "Anger" stage.

- Once market erosion becomes severe, a Counter-Positioned incumbent comes under tremendous pressure to do something; at the same time, they face great pressure to not upset the apple cart of the legacy business model. A frequent outcome of this duality? Let's call it dabbling: the incumbent puts a toe in the water, somehow, but refuses to commit in a way that meaningfully answers the challenge.

- Counter-Positioning often underlies situations in which the following developments are jointly observed:
  - For the challenger
    - Rapid share gains
    - Strong profitability (or at least the promise of it)
  - For the incumbent
    - Share loss
    - Inability to counter the entrant's moves
    - Eventual management shake-up (s)
    - Capitulation, often occuring too late

The Challenger's Advantage

An entrenched incumbent with established Power is formidable—this is axiomatic. Unless the incumbent is incompetent over an extended period of time, challenging it is most often a loser's game, and playing that game is no fun—AMD's long and enervating battle to emerge from the shadow of Intel yields a case in point.

That said, there are fighting styles which turn the contest on its head by converting strength into weakness. Think of Muhammed Ali's defeat of the intimidating George Foreman with his improvised Rope-A-Dope: Ali relied on Foreman's straight-ahead style and confidence to lure him into strength-sapping flurries.

Such reversals are rare in business, because contests typically take place over extended periods and with great thoughtfulness on all sides. Even a momentary lapse by an incumbent won't present a sufficient opening. The only bet worthwhile for a challenger is one in which *even if the incumbent plays its best game*, it can be taken off the board. A competent Counter-Positioned challenger must take advantage of the strengths of the incumbent, as it is this strength which molds the Barrier, collateral damage.

Counter-Positioning Leverage

For Counter-Positioning, the Competitor Position element of Power is simply binary: you have adopted the heterodox business model. The Industry Economics aspect of Power refers to the central characteristics of this model: it must be superior, and it must cause the expectation of perceived collateral damage.

Figure 3.5: Power Intensity Determinants

	Industry Economics	**Competitive Position**
Scale Economies	Scale economy intensity	Relative scale
Network Economies	Network effect intensity	Absolute difference in installed base
Counter-Positioning	New business model superiority + collateral damage to old	Binary: entrant—new model; incumbent—old model

Appendix 3.1: Derivation of Surplus Leader Margin for Counter-Positioning

To calibrate the intensity of Power, I ask the question "What governs profitability of the company with Power (S) when prices are such that the company with no Power (W) makes no profit at all?" In the case of Counter-Positioning (CP), the incumbent is W and the challenger is S.

Both business models are strictly variable cost: Profits $\equiv \pi = (P - c)\, Q$

With $P \equiv$ price per unit

   $c \equiv$ variable cost per unit

   $Q \equiv$ unit volume

There are two business models: Old $\equiv$ O and New $\equiv$ N

N's superior business model => $^{N}c < {}^{O}c$; N cannibalizes O via $^{N}P < {}^{O}P$. W faces the choice of whether to enter N or not.

Surplus leader margin (SLM) is the margin the company with Power can earn while pricing is such that the margin of the weaker firm is zero. SLM is an indicator of the intensity of Power. The surplus indicated (if positive) gives S the opportunity for profits and/or Power position enforcement. In the cases of Network Economies and Scale Economies, the scale leader is S, so SLM indicates retaliatory latitude in protecting market share. In the case of CP, S is the challenger, and Power position enforcement involves diminishing the likelihood that W, the incumbent, will enter N to battle S. Such enforcement involves increasing the collateral damage.

SLM in CP will be the S's margin when the incremental profitability for W of deciding to enter N is zero.

For simplicity I will look at this as a single-period problem, although in the real world the businesses will likely be evaluating a number of periods.

So for collateral damage to just cancel out the gains to W from entering N:

Note that I will drop the W, S notation since collateral damage only refers to W's economics.

$SLM \Rightarrow {}^N\pi + \Delta^O\pi = 0$ where $\Delta^O\pi$ is the change in W's O business' profits *induced* by their entry into N

$CP \Rightarrow {}^N\text{margin} * {}^N\text{revenue} + {}^O\text{margin} * \Delta^O\text{revenue} = 0$

$\quad {}^Nm * [{}^NP * {}^NQ] + {}^Om * [{}^OP * \Delta^OQ] = 0$ where $Q \equiv$ unit volume and $m \equiv$ profit margin

$\quad {}^Nm * [{}^NP * {}^NQ] = - {}^Om * [{}^OP * \Delta^OQ]$

$\quad {}^Nm = {}^Om * [{}^OP / {}^NP] * [-\Delta^OQ / {}^NQ]$

Let $\delta \equiv$ W's induced cannibalization ratio of O into N: $\delta = -\Delta^OQ / {}^NQ$

So $\boxed{\mathbf{SLM = {}^Om * [{}^OP / {}^NP] * \delta}}$

So SLM > 0 combined with the earlier conditions of ${}^NP < {}^OP$ and ${}^Nc < {}^Oc$ characterize the Milk case of CP. Both a Benefit and a Barrier are evident.

Let me comment on the implications of this specification:

- If $\Delta^OQ = 0$. This means that W anticipates that their entry into N will cause no additional volumes losses in their base business O.

    o Then $\delta = 0$.

    o This would result in SLM = 0 so there is no CP.

    o What is going on, of course, is that there is simply no collateral damage.

    o Thus a commonly observed behavior is that Counter-Positioned incumbents will seek customer segments in which they induce no additional loss of O customers by offering N.

- For example, a *Financial Times* article of Oct. 24, 2015: *Walt Disney's most beloved characters and stories are going digital in a new streaming service that launches in the UK next month.*

  DisneyLife bundles books and music with its animated and live action films, making Disney the biggest media company yet to stream its content directly to consumers online.

  Disney will expand the service across Europe next year, with the goal of launching in France, Spain, Italy and Germany, and would add content as it becomes available, the company said.

  ...It has no plans to bring the service to the US, its biggest market, because of potential overlaps with the many agreements it has with cable and satellite companies that distribute its film and television content.

- If $\delta < 1$ (the unit gains in N are more than offset by the losses in O for W).

  - CP is unlikely. For CP, the margins would have to be attractive enough in N to offset both the lower prices in N and the volume losses.

  - Thus the incumbent would need to anticipate volume gains in N which more than offset the cannibalization of O volume induced by their entry into N.

- One of the ironies of CP is that the higher the incumbent's margins, the higher the SLM. This of course simply reflects that W has more to lose by erosion of their O business. CP therefore can present a potent challenge to an entrenched highly successful incumbent.

- The potential for cognitive bias (History's Slave) can be usefully explored by noting the elements of the SLM equation. In considering entry into N, the incumbent will often exhibit a cognitive bias that raises their expected δ, and thus increases SLM.

  - They have more certainty regarding $\Delta^O Q$ than $^N Q$ so they often understate $^N Q$. For example, someone within W who wishes to push ahead and enter N is often incented not to promise too much.

- ○ Thus this creates a cognitive skew toward CP.

- The potential for agency effects (Job Security) can also be looked at through the lens of the SLM equation.

  - ○ Example 1. An important decision influencer is the division head responsible for the O business.

    - ▪ The O business has been the corporation's bread and butter, so this person's voice carries a lot of weight.

    - ▪ However, the N business results are attributed to another division or group.

    - ▪ So using my example from this chapter, imagine that the active fund managers would get no credit for the assets under management in the newly formed passive funds, a quite realistic assumption.

    - ▪ This arrangement assures that $^{N}Q = 0$ for this individual (group), and this means $\delta = \infty$ assuring CP.

  - ○ Example 2. At the CEO level, compensation may be set in a way that places emphasis on near-in results (this year, for example). Although I have used a single-period formulation in this appendix, the real calculation should be an NPV, and, as I have discussed, out years weigh heavily on this. The agency effects may lead to lower weights to these out years and, as I will discuss below, collateral damage tends to become less and less likely to be met as you go forward in time.

- The reader should also keep in mind that the agency and cognitive effects in CP are not mutually exclusive with the Milk case. In fact, they are frequently additive: all three effects operating at the same time.

- Dynamic effects

  - ○ As you move forward in time, δ tends to decline, reducing Power intensity (and perhaps eliminating CP altogether).

- The reason for this is that as the aggregate cumulative cannibalization of O by N increases, ^{N}Q tends to go up because the opportunity overall for N is larger as it becomes proven and known, and $|\Delta^{O}Q|$ tends to go down as the expected loss in O business is seen to come primarily from the challenger's incursions, rather than that induced by W's entry into N.

- Also the agency and cognitive skews toward fulfilling the collateral damage condition tend to diminish over time as the uncertainty surrounding the threat of N diminishes and the agents aligned with O in W tend to lose credibility and influence.

- Since δ tends to decline, SLM declines and the collateral damage may be insufficient to deter W's entry into N. This is the capitulation point mentioned in the chapter.

- I understand that this specification is highly stylized. Even so, the future profit calculations in corporations tend not to be theoretically complex, so even this stylized representation may capture much of what is going on.

- Tactically, it is probably a good idea for S to set prices at first such that ^{N}m is very low—much lower than ^{O}m.

  - ^{N}m is usually observable by W as is ^{N}P, whereas δ is not.

  - So if $[^{N}P/^{O}P]$ is quite small, then W has to be quite optimistic about a low cannibalization rate (δ) to lead to an SLM > 0 thus creating CP.

  - A special case is one in which S offers N at first for ^{N}P such that ^{N}m < 0. This makes $[^{N}m/^{O}m]$ < 0 and assures the collateral damage condition is met for the periods of this pricing. Since ^{N}P is observed but S's motivation is not, W may well discount the possibility that S will eventually raise prices such that ^{N}m > 0 whereas S can know this, assuming they are a price leader.

CHAPTER 4
SWITCHING COSTS
ADDICTION

Agony at HP

SAP is the world's leading supplier of enterprise resource planning software (ERP). Users rely on this software to collect and analyze data essential for running a modern corporation: accounting data, sales tracking, manufacturing management and so on. Despite SAP's success in ERP, the company is no poster-child for customer satisfaction. According to Geoff Scott, CEO of America's SAP Users' Group, "As a former CIO, one of the biggest and most consistent complaints I heard from my line of business partners was the complexity and difficulty of the SAP user experience."[32] A recent Compuware study[33] of 588 SAP customers in Europe and the US found that 43% were unhappy with SAP response times across all components. Nearly all felt that SAP performance problems would result in financial risks, and 50% felt unable to predict SAP performance. Yet another survey[34] of more than 1,000 customers found that 89% expected to continue paying the annual maintenance fees for SAP in the near future. Why would customers continue to pay for a product they so dislike? It seems as though the old adage "No one ever got fired for buying IBM" has been supplanted by "No one ever got fired for sticking with SAP."

The explanation for this paradox lies in the Power type covered in this chapter: Switching Costs. A simple example is Apple's hold on its iTunes customers. Apple downloads come in a proprietary format, so in switching to another program, Apple customers forfeit their prior purchases. This is an unattractive prospect, which accounts for why so many customers stay locked in.

The ERP model offers a more complex and larger-scale illustration. The decision to replace any ERP carries high cost. Once ERP is integrated into a client's business, employees have sunk the cost of learning to use this system, relationships have been established with the new service team to solve problems, and investments have been made in compatible software to customize the system to the client's needs. Once done, changing that only comes at an extraordinarily high cost: the time and effort to research competitive offerings, the purchase cost of a replacement ERP system, all the complementary software, transferring the data, retraining employees, forming new relationships, and risking interruption of services and loss of data during the transition from one system to another.

To illustrate the onerous Switching Costs a firm would have to worry about, consider what happened when Hewlett Packard migrated their North American server sales divisions ($7.5 billion revenue at the time) to SAP. This followed a corporate directive for an enterprise-wide ERP implementation, meaning the division had no choice but to bear the costs, whatever they might be.

Christina Hanger was Hewlett-Packard (HP)'s Senior Vice President of American Operations in May 2004.[35] She was already an old hand at SAP migrations, having already overseen five of them at HP following their acquisition of Compaq, and this experience guided her budgeting: three weeks to accommodate changeover of the legacy order-entry system to the SAP system, plus three weeks of extra server inventory. Hanger also commandeered additional HP factory capacity in Omaha to accommodate unforeseen production demands that might arise during the switchover. Simply put: she was well prepared.

Even her careful preparation was insufficient, however.

> Starting when the system went live at the beginning of June and continuing throughout the rest of the month, as many as 20 percent of customer orders for servers stopped dead in their tracks between the legacy order-entry system and the SAP system.[36]

HP was not the only company selling servers—customers could easily turn to Dell or IBM. So, as backlog piled up, HP started to lose business. In her conference call with analysts HP CEO Carly Fiorina later stated that this snafu resulted in a $160M financial hit. The HP experience perfectly exemplifies not only the high Switching Costs (considerably more than the software itself) an ERP migrator can expect, but also the intimidating uncertainty which surrounds the planning for such a migration.

SAP's paradoxical combination of high retention and low satisfaction reflects the economic reality of a software product of great value to a corporation but one that also comes with high Switching Costs. Once a customer has bought in, they are hopelessly hooked, enabling SAP to then reap the rewards of a future stream of revenues for annual maintenance charges, upgrades, add-on services, software and consulting. More, a company like SAP, profiting from the indenture of its clients, has all incentive to hike the prices of such services. The continued climb of SAP's stock price, shown below in Figure 4.1, testifies to the vitality and endurance afforded by the business model born of such reliance.[37]

Figure 4.1: SAP Stock Price[38]

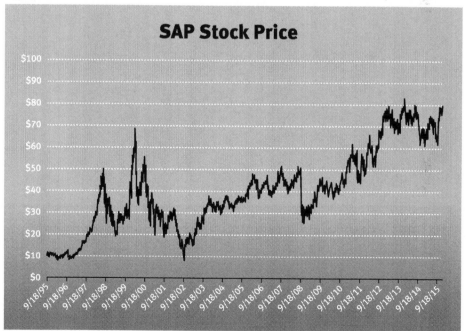

Switching Costs on the 7 Powers

Switching Costs arise when a consumer values compatibility across multiple purchases from a specific firm over time. These can include repeat purchases of the same product or purchases of complementary goods.[39]

> *Benefit.* A company that has embedded Switching Costs for its current customers can charge higher prices than competitors for equivalent products or services.[40] This benefit only accrues to the Power holder in selling follow-on products to their *current* customers; they hold no Benefit with potential customers and there is no Benefit if there are no follow-on products.

> *Barrier.* To offer an equivalent product,[41] competitors must compensate customers for Switching Costs. The firm that has previously roped in the customer, then, can set or adjust prices in a way that puts their potential rival at a cost disadvantage, rendering such a challenge distinctly unattractive. Thus, as with Scale Economies and Network Economies, the Barrier arises from the unattractive cost/benefit of share gains for the challenger.

With this understanding, I can now place Switching Costs on the 7 Powers Chart:

Figure 4.2: Switching Costs in the 7 Powers

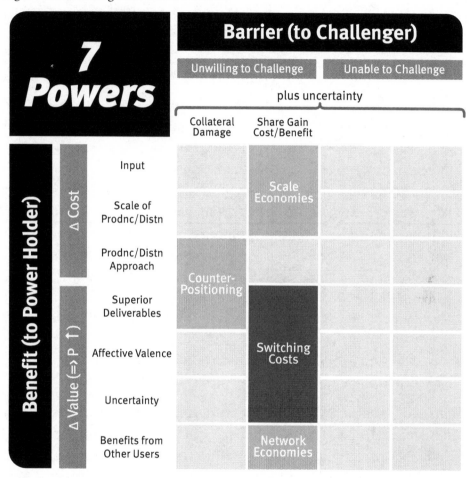

Switching Costs definition:

> *The value loss expected by a customer that would be incurred from switching to an alternate supplier for additional purchases.*

Types of Switching Costs

Switching Costs can be divided into three broad groups:[42]

Financial. Financial Switching Costs include those which are transparently monetary from the outset. For ERP, these would include the purchase of both a new database and the sum total of its complementary applications.

Procedural. Procedural Switching Costs are somewhat murkier but no less persuasive. They stem from the loss of familiarity with the product or from the the risk and uncertainty associated with the adoption of a new product. When employees have invested time and effort to learn the particulars of how to use a certain product, there can be a significant cost to retraining them in a different system. In the case of SAP, applications exist for a wide array of enterprise functions. This means that there are employees in human resources, sales and marketing, procurement, accounting, not to mention managers across these many divisions, who have all learned how to create reports based on the SAP system and its complementary software. Such a system-switch breeds organizational discontent by forcing many within the ranks of the organization to change their daily routines.

Furthermore, procedural changes open the door for errors. With databases, these are particularly costly, since they involve the totality of the customer's information. Even when a competitor provides services and programs to help mitigate such difficulties of transition, these often prove costly and imperfect.

Relational. Relational Switching Costs are those tolls which would result from the breaking of emotional bonds built up through use of the product and through interactions with other users and service providers. Often a customer establishes close, beneficial relationships with the provider's sales and service teams. Such familiarity, ease of communication and mutual positive feelings can create resistance to the prospect of severing those ties and switching to another vendor. Additionally, if the customer has developed affection for the product and their identity as a user, or if they enjoy the camaraderie which exists amongst a community of like users, they may shrink from the prospect of switching identities and abandoning that community.[43]

Switching Costs Multipliers

Switching Costs are a non-exclusive Power type: all players can enjoy their benefits. IBM and Oracle are competitors to SAP, and they also benefit from high customer retention rates and Switching Costs. As a market matures, the Benefit of Switching Costs becomes transparent to all players and they are able to calculate the value of an acquired customer. More often than not this leads to enhanced competition to grab new customers, which arbitrages out the Benefit for new customer acquisitions.[44] So the major value contribution comes from capturing customers before such value-destroying pricing arbitrage transpires.

Switching Costs offer no Benefit if no additional related sales are made to the customer. To assure that such additional sales take place, one tactic might be to develop more and more add-on products. This has been SAP's tack, as seen from this Wikipedia list of the company's offerings.[45]

Figure 4.3: SAP Product Offerings[46]

SAP Advanced Planner and Optimizer (APO)	SAP Human Resource Management Systems (HRMS)
SAP Analytics	SAP Success Factors
SAP Advanced Business Application Programming (ABAP)	SAP Internet Transaction Server (ITS)
SAP Apparel and Footwear Solution (AFS)	SAP Incentive and Commission Management (ICM)
SAP Business Information Warehouse (BW)	SAP Knowledge Warehouse (KW)
SAP Business Intelligence (BI)	SAP Manufacturing
SAP Catalog Content Management ()	SAP Master Data Management MDM)
SAP Convergent Charging (CC)	SAP Rapid Deployment Solutions (RDS)
SAP Enterprise Buyer Professional (EBP)	SAP Service and Asset Management
SAP Enterprise Learning	SAP Solutions for mobile businesses
SAP Portal (EP)	SAP Solution Composer
SAP Exchange Infrastructure (XI) (From release 7.0 onwards, SAP XI has been renamed as SAP Process Integration [SAP PI])	SAP Strategic Enterprise Management (SEM)
	SAP Test Data Migration Server (TDMS)
SAP Extended Warehouse Management (EWM)	SAP Training and Event Management (TEM)
SAP GRC (Governance, Risk and Compliance)	SAP NetWeaver Application Server (Web AS)
SAP EHSM (Environment Health Safety Management)	SAP xApps
Enterprise Central Component (ECC)	SAP Supply Chain Performance Management (SCPM)
SAP HANA (formerly known as High-performance Analytics Appliance)	SAP Sustainability Performance Management (SUPM)

Acquisitions significantly accelerate product line extensions, too, serving as a sort of outsourced development. This too has been part of SAP's playbook, as proven by their ambitious acquisition program.[47]

Figure 4.4: Number of SAP Acquisitions by Year[48]

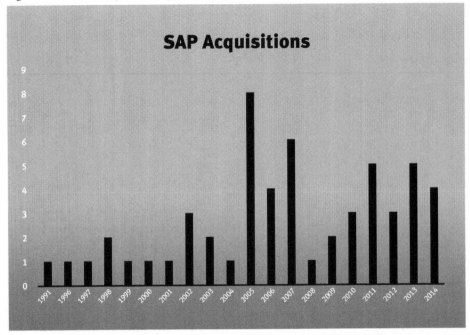

The building of such product portfolios can serve to boost all three categories of Switching Costs. Not only does it extend the revenue coverage of the Switching Costs (Financial), but it often increases their intensity by making the prospect of disentanglement more and more forbidding (Procedural). A high level of integration into customer operations, and the extensive training that demands, can also further disincentivize such disentanglement. This sort of training also has the potential of building emotional bonds to the current supplier (Relational).

Switching Costs: Industry Economics and Competitive Position

As noted before, Switching Costs are a non-exclusive Power: their benefits are available to all players. So the intensity of Switching Costs derives from "Industry

Economics," those conditions faced equally by all players. The potential benefits accrue only if you have a customer, so the competitive position component of Switching Costs is binary: you either have the customer, or you do not.

I should note that such advantages can be swept away by tectonic shifts in technology. ERP firms know well this lesson; that's why SAP and Oracle are presently doing their best to make certain they are not leapfrogged by cloud-based applications.

Importantly, too, Switching Costs can pave the path for other Powers as well. Connecting users and building a large supply of complementary goods may generate Network Effects. Or if the product preference of users already tethered by Switching Costs spills over to a wider pool of potential customers, you could find yourself enjoying the effects of Branding.

Figure 4.5: Power Intensity Determinants

	Industry Economics	*Competitive Position*
Scale Economies	Scale economy intensity	Relative scale
Network Economies	Intensity of network effect	Absolute difference in installed base
Counter-Positioning	New business model superiority + collateral damage to old	Binary: entrant—new model; incumbent—old model
Switching Costs	Magnitude (intensity) of switching costs	Number of current customers

Appendix 4.1: Surplus Leader Margin for Switching Costs

S is the strong company and W the weak company. In this case the "weak company" is the company not having the customer.

$_sQ$ consumers have already adopted S's product. I will now examine the benefit that accrues to S due to sales of subsequent products to $_sQ$.

Suppose for simplicity that the utility of the subsequent product is the same for both firms. S is able to charge a price premium due to switching costs Δ:

$$_sP = \Delta + {_w}P$$

Also for simplicity, assume that there are no fixed costs to production.

$$\text{Profit} \equiv \pi = [P - c]\ Q$$
$$\text{with} \quad P \equiv \text{price}$$
$$c \equiv \text{variable cost per unit}$$
$$Q \equiv \text{units produced per time period}$$

As an indication of leverage, assess:

What governs S's margins if P is set $\ni {_w}\pi = 0$?

$$_w\pi = 0 \Rightarrow \qquad 0 = ({_w}P - c)\ {_s}Q \qquad \Rightarrow {_w}P = c$$

Δ is the Switching Cost per unit

S can charge a premium, so $_sP = \Delta + c$

$$\therefore \qquad {_s}\pi = [(\Delta + c) - c]\ {_s}Q$$
$$_s\pi = \Delta\ {_s}Q$$

$$\boxed{\textbf{SLM} = \boldsymbol{\Delta}}$$

Industry Economics: Δ
Competitive Position: $_sQ$

CHAPTER 5
BRANDING
FEELING GOOD

In 2005, *Good Morning America* purchased a diamond ring at Tiffany & Co. for $16,600 and one of similar size and cut at Costco for $6,600. They then asked Martin Fuller, a reputable gemologist and appraiser, to assess the rings' values. Fuller assessed the Costco ring at $8,000 plus setting costs, more than $2,000 above the selling price. "It's a little bit of a surprise. You wouldn't normally consider a fine diamond to be found in a general store like Costco...."[49] Fuller assessed the Tiffany ring at $10,500 plus setting costs at a non-brand-name retailer.

The result is hardly idiosyncratic. Compared to the more generic Blue Nile online offering, Tiffany's prices are nearly double.

Figure 5.1: Price Comparisons for Engagement Rings

Seller and Product, 1 carat	Starting Price in US Dollars
Tiffany: The Tiffany Setting (I VS2)	$12,000
Cartier: Solitaire 1895 (H VS2)	$14,800
DeBeers: Signature	$12,200
Blue Nile: Classic 6-prong (I VS2)	$6,697

How is it that Tiffany can successfully charge a substantial price premium over other sellers of what is a demonstrably identical offering? Fuller described it this way:

> "You got exactly what they said you were getting. Anything that is brand-name and has developed a reputation that Tiffany has developed, they've earned it over the years for quality control. You can go there [and] you don't have to think twice about your purchase. And you pay for that."

Direct customer sentiments make this propensity even more evident—for example, a prospective fiancé's post on an online forum: "Is a Tiffany engagement ring worth the cost?"

#54
12-03-2009, 8:43PM

User X
Location: Encinitas, CA

I bought Tiffany and knew I was getting soaked. Didn't matter — happy then and would do it again (in fact, I upgraded her wedding band to matching channel diamonds years later.)

My priority was to buy the best from the best without any doubt of quality/certification/etc. Size was not important. I wanted indisputable perfect to match her. We're not showy people and have never played up the fact the rings are from Tiffany's. It was more appropriate to me to buy a reasonalble size stone and know with quiet confidence that the ring is timeless — not a cheap knock-off or guady bauble.

The other thing that I was mindful of was that someday (like when I'm dead) one of my grandchildren will inherit it. Part of the rationale for me was "instant heirloom." One of these future grandkids is going to think "Damn, grandpa was ****ing cool!"

Last edited by User X; 12-03-2009 at 8:46 PM.

Another response to a similar question on a different forum emphasizes the extra value imparted by the recipient's awareness of the ring's provenance:

Tiffany's position may be enviable, but getting there was a long, arduous journey. The company was founded in 1837 and has long cultivated a reputation for high-quality jewelry. They first gained world recognition by winning awards for their silver craftsmanship in 1867 at the Paris World's Fair and continued to win awards at subsequent World's Fairs. In 1878, Tiffany acquired and cut the famed Tiffany Diamond, and in 1886, Tiffany introduced a diamond engagement ring with the Tiffany Setting, comprised of six prongs to separate the diamond from the band, in contrast to the bezel setting common at the time. The brand has become a standard for wealth and luxury.

Over this long history, Tiffany has carefully curated its image. Packaging provides a famous case in point. Tiffany's website touts the message conveyed by its signature Blue Box:

> Glimpsed on a busy street or resting in the palm of a hand, Tiffany
> Blue Boxes make hearts beat faster and epitomize Tiffany's great
> heritage of elegance, exclusivity and flawless craftsmanship.[50]

This wording is hardly casual:

- "Heritage" implies a long and positive history of doing the same thing (in this case, creating elegant, exclusive and flawless jewelry).

- "Elegance" designates a particular aesthetic design which consumers can consistently expect from the product despite repeated changes in lead designers and collections.

- "Exclusivity" hints that the Tiffany product can only be attained by those willing to pay for the very best. It also suggests that only Tiffany, and no competitor, can provide this type of craftsmanship.

- "Flawless" assures the customer that over this long history Tiffany has repeatedly created perfect products, meaning buyers face no uncertainty as to the quality of the jewelry.

Tiffany's success is evidenced by the fact that, although the Blue Box comes free with a purchase, it carries a standalone monetary value.

Figure 5.1: Completed eBay Auction for Tiffany Box

Genuine Tiffany & Co. Empty Engagement Ring Box, Bag, Tiffany & Co

Item condition:	**Pre-owned**
Ended:	May 27, 2015, 12:22PM
Winning bid:	**US $122.50** [33 bids]
	Located in United States

Seller information

100% Positive feedback

+ Follow this seller

See other items

Tiffany's pricing advantage drives strong differential margins (in the Fundamental Equation of Strategy). This is implied by the radically superior profit margins they achieve relative to Blue Nile over the last decade:

Figure 5.2: Annual Profit Margins for Blue Nile and Tiffany [51]

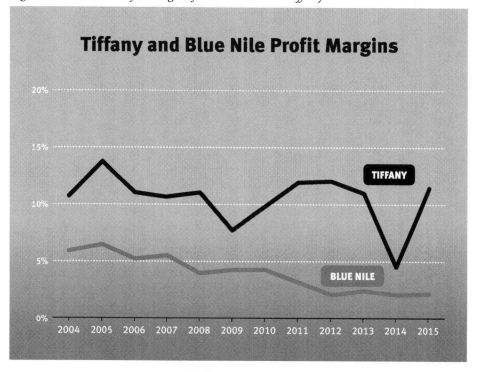

The value thus created underlies their $10B market capitalization, and their steady, rising stock price demonstrates the durability of investors' expectation:

Figure 5.3: Tiffany Stock Price[52]

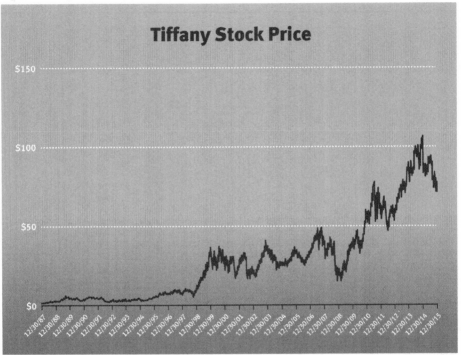

Branding

Tiffany's Power lies in Branding. Branding is an asset that communicates information and evokes positive emotions in the customer, leading to an increased willingness to pay for the product.

Benefit. A business with Branding is able to charge a higher price for its offering due to one or both of these two reasons:

1. *Affective valence.* The built-up associations with the brand elicit good feelings about the offering, distinct from the objective value of the good. For example, Safeway's cola may be indistinguishable from Coke's in a blind taste test, but even after revealing the result, the taste tester remains willing to pay more for Coke.

2. *Uncertainty reduction.* A customer attains "peace of mind" knowing that the branded product will be as just as expected. Consider another example: Bayer aspirin. Search for aspirin on Amazon.com and you will see a 200 count of Bayer 325 mg. aspirin for $9.47 side-by-side with a 500 count of Kirkland 325 mg. aspirin for $10.93. So Bayer has a price per tablet premium of 117%. Some customers still would prefer the Bayer because of diminished uncertainty: Bayer's long history of consistency makes customers more confident that they are getting exactly what they want. Note that the Benefit from Branding does not depend on prior ownership, as with Switching Costs.

Barrier. A strong brand can only be created over a lengthy period of reinforcing actions (*hysteresis*), which itself serves as the key Barrier. Again, Tiffany has cultivated its brand name for more than a century. What's more, copycats face daunting uncertainty in initiating Branding: a long investment runway with no assurance of an eventual path to significant affective valence. Efforts to mimic another brand run the risk of trademark infringement actions as well with their attendant costs and unclear outcomes.

With this understanding, I can now place Branding on the 7 Powers Chart:

Figure 5.4: Branding in the 7 Powers

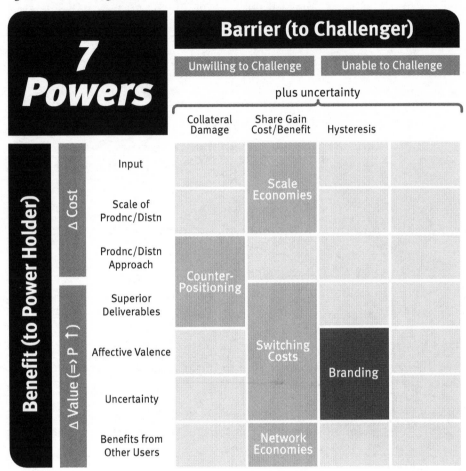

Branding definition:

The durable attribution of higher value to an objectively identical offering that arises from historical information about the seller.

Branding—Challenges and Characteristics

Brand Dilution. Firms require focus and diligence to guide Branding over time and ensure that the reputation created remains consistent in the valences it generates. Hence, the biggest pitfall lies in diminishing the brand by releasing products which deviate from, or damage, the brand image.

Seeking higher "down market" volumes can reduce affective valence by damaging the aura of exclusivity, weakening positive associations with the product. For example, Halston rose to fame in the 1970s as a high-end design standard for women's clothing. However, when Halston accepted $1 billion from lower-end retailer J.C. Penney to expand into affordable fashion lines for the mass consumer, Bergdorf Goodman dropped the label in order to protect their brand. The J.C. Penney line was a failure, and the Halston name never recaptured its previously enviable Branding.

I stated earlier that Branding's Barrier is hysteresis and uncertainty. Dilution threatens Branding Power because it can "reset the hysteresis clock," forcing a company to restart the slow and uncertain process of building affective valence. The Halston experience serves as a persuasive case in point.

Counterfeiting. Since it is the label, not the product, that bestows Branding Power, counterfeiters may try to free-ride by falsely associating a powerful brand with their product. Because Branding relies upon repeated positive interactions with consumers, counterfeiters who flood the market with inconsistent offerings can gradually undermine it. For instance, in 2013 Tiffany sued Costco for intimating to shoppers that they sold Tiffany jewelery; the company had previously sued eBay for facilitating the sale of counterfeits. A press release to investors after the filing of the 2013 suit explicitly noted that, "Tiffany has never sold nor would it ever sell its fine jewelry through an off-price warehouse retailer like Costco."[53]

Changing consumer preferences. Over time, customer preferences may vary in a way that undermines the value of Branding. Nintendo developed a brand for family-friendly video games. However, as the gaming demographic evolved from predominantly children to adults, there was a shift in demand for more mature games. Nintendo's Branding did not extend to this segment with the attendant negative impact. In terms of the Fundamental Equation of Strategy, the attractive differential margins ($\overline{m}$) achieved in the M_0 of the children's segment would elude Nintendo in the adult segment.[54] Problem is, the qualities that make Branding a Power also make it hard to change; the considerable risk is dilution or brand destruction.

Geographic boundaries. The affective valence may apply in one region but not another. For example, for many years, Sony enjoyed a Branding advantage with its televisions in the United States. In Japan, however, it enjoyed no such advantage, thus preventing it from enjoying premium pricing over rivals such as Panasonic.

Narrowness. To clear the high hurdle of Power, Branding in the context of Power Dynamics is a much more restricted concept than in marketing. For example, even if "brand recognition" is very high, there may not be Branding Power. In instances like this, it could actually be Scale Economies creating heightened brand awareness. For example, Coca Cola can sponsor Super Bowl ads while RC Crown Cola cannot because the ad cost is only justifiable for an entity of Coca Cola's size. A strategist would gravely err in classifying this as Branding. RC could make all the right Branding moves and still be at the same disadvantage due to relative scale.

Non-exclusivity. Note that Branding is a non-exclusive type of Power. Indeed, a direct competitor might have an equally impactful brand that targets the same customers (e.g., Prada and Luis Vuitton and Hermès). All competitors with brand Power, however, still will earn returns superior to those of the competitor with no Branding.

Type of Good. Only certain types of goods have Branding potential (more on this in the Appendix on Surplus Leader Margin) as they must clear two conditions:

1. **Magnitude:** the promise of eventually justifying a significant price premium.
   a. Business-to-business goods typically fail to exhibit meaningful affective valence price premia, since most purchasers are only

concerned with objective deliverables. Consumer goods, in particular those associated with a sense of identity, tend to have the purchasing decision more driven by affective valence. Here's the reason: in order to associate with an identity, there must be some way to signal the exclusion of alternative identities.

b. For Branding Power derived from uncertainty reduction, the customer's higher willingness to pay is driven by high perceived costs of uncertainty relative to the cost of the good. Such products tend to be those associated with bad tail events: safety, medicine, food, transport, etc. Branded medicine formulations, for example, are identical to those of generics, yet garner a significantly higher price.

2. **Duration:** a long enough amount of time to achieve such magnitude. If the requisite duration is not present, the Benefit attained will fall prey to normal arbitraging behavior.

Branding: Industry Economics and Competitive Position

To finish this chapter, I place Branding Power on my Industry Economics/ Competitive Position table. In the case of Branding, I assume all costs are marginal, so the zero challenger profit price equals marginal costs. The value the leader offers is greater than this by the brand value it offers, and I assume they can charge a higher price. As a consequence:

$$^S\text{Margin} = 1 - 1/B(t)$$

where $B(t) \equiv$ brand value as a multiple of the weaker firm's price
$t \equiv$ units of time since the initial investment in brand

Industry economics define the function $B(t)$ (specified in the appendix) and determine the magnitude and sustainability of leverage. Time t represents the competitive position that S has relative to W in developing brand power.

Figure 5.5: Power Intensity Determinants

	Industry Economics	*Competitive Position*
Scale Economies	Scale economy intensity	Relative scale
Network Economies	Intensity of network effect	Absolute difference in installed base
Counter-Positioning	New business model superiority + collateral damage to old	Binary: entrant—new model; incumbent—old model
Switching Costs	Magnitude (intensity) of switching costs	Number of current customers
Branding	Time constant and potential magnitude of Branding effect	Duration of brand investing

Appendix 5.1: Surplus Leader Margin for Branding

To calibrate the intensity of Power, I ask the question "What governs profitability of the company with Power (S) when prices are such that the company with no Power (W) makes no profit at all?"

S is the strong company (the one with Branding Power) and W the weak company.

To derive a formula for SLM for Branding, I need to specify what determines the upper envelope of the price premium enjoyed by the strong firm (S). B(t) is that specification.

$$B(t) = Z/(1 + (z-1)e^{-Ft}) * D_t * U_t$$

B (t) $\equiv$ branding price multiple at time t

Z $\equiv$ maximum potential branding multiple for this good type, Z > 2

F $\equiv$ brand cycle time compression factor, F > 0

D_t $\equiv$ brand dilution at time t, $0 \leq D \leq 1$

U_t $\equiv$ brand underinvestment at time t $0 \leq U \leq 1$

B(t) is an increasing function of t, reflecting the reality that Branding requires action over time to be increased. The logistic function was chosen to reflect the reinforcing aspect of Branding investment, while allowing diminishing marginal returns over time. The particular form specified above for B(t) ensures that B(t)=1 at t=0 by adjusting the location parameter as a function of F and Z. When F is larger, the logistic curve steepens and the brand cycle time is shorter. When F is smaller, the logistic curve grows shallower and the brand cycle time is longer. As seen in Figure 5.6, D = 1 if there is no brand dilution, and U = 1 if there is no brand underinvestment; otherwise, D and U reduce the brand multiple in a given period by some fraction.

Time determines competitive position, because it determines the ability of a competitor starting at time t = 0 to catch up to the strong firm at time t = t. Z, and F (i.e., B()) determines industry position. As seen in Figure 5.6, the weak competitor falls further and further behind as the length of the life cycle grows;

so too then does it become harder and harder for that weak competitor to catch up to the strong firm. The sustainability of the brand depends on the shape of the $B(t)$ function relative to $B(0)$ for all t in the case of the weakest competitor with no Branding, and an alternative $B'(t)$ function (i.e. an alternative F') and alternative t for another competitor.

For simplicity, assume that there are no fixed costs to production.

$$\text{Profit} \equiv \pi = [P - c]\, Q$$

$$\text{with} \quad P \equiv \text{price}$$
$$c \equiv \text{marginal cost per unit}$$
$$Q \equiv \text{units produced per time period}$$

As an indication of leverage, assess:

What governs S's margins if P is set $\ni {}_W\pi = 0$?

$${}_W\pi = 0 \Rightarrow \quad 0 = ({}_WP - c)\, {}_SQ \Rightarrow {}_WP = c$$

S can charge a premium as a multiple of ${}_WP$, so ${}_SP = B(t){*}c$

$$\therefore \quad {}_S\pi = [B(t){*}c - c]\, {}_SQ = [(B(t)-1){*}c]\, {}_SQ$$
$${}_S\pi = (B(t)-1)c\, {}_SQ$$

$${}_S\text{Margin} = (B(t)-1)c\, {}_SQ/(B(t)c\, {}_SQ) = 1 - 1/B(t)$$

So $\boxed{\textbf{SLM} = 1 - 1/B(t)}$

where the function B() represents the industry economics defining the magnitude and sustainability of leverage through Z and F, respectively, and t represents the competitive position that S has relative to W in developing Branding Power.

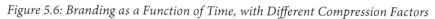
Figure 5.6: Branding as a Function of Time, with Different Compression Factors

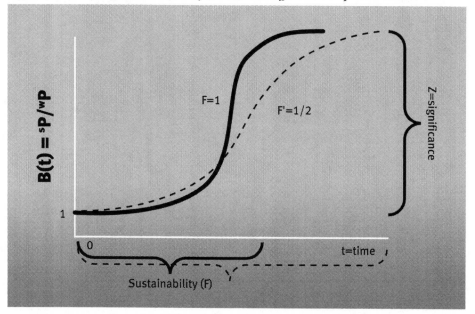

CHAPTER 6
CORNERED RESOURCE
MINE ALL MINE

To Infinity and Beyond

On November 22, 1995, Pixar's *Toy Story* premiered. This was a hold-your-breath moonshot: the first computer-animated feature film, Pixar's first feature film, and John Lasseter's feature directorial debut. One could not help but be reminded of Walt Disney's 1937 bet-the-company gambit, *Snow White and the Seven Dwarfs*. And like Disney's earlier effort, *Toy Story* soared: with a production budget of only $30M, it went on to realize a worldwide box office take of over $350M, while winning Pixar and Disney deserved critical acclaim. Critic Roger Ebert rhapsodized:

> "Watching the film, I felt I was in at the dawn of a new era of movie animation, which draws on the best of cartoons and reality, creating a world somewhere in between, where space not only bends but snaps, crackles and pops."[55]

This triumph was foundational. It was *Toy Story* that enabled Pixar to go public in November of 1995, orchestrated by Steve Jobs as the irrepressible roadshow master of ceremonies. As NASDAQ PIXR, the frequent existential threats facing the fledgling studio receded into memory and Pixar's negotiating position with its finance and distribution partner, Disney, transformed.

Figure 6.1: The First Ten Pixar Films

©Disney·Pixar

But what came next did not at all follow the Disney script of its animated films. Whereas Disney struggled to repeat the success of *Snow White and the Seven Dwarfs*, Pixar followed up with *A Bug's Life* in 1998 and *Toy Story 2* in 1999. Both were stunning artistic and commercial successes, signaling the start of the most compelling run in the history of the movie business. Who does not have warm recollections of the early Pixar films of Figure 6.1, as well as those they would produce subsequently?

Pixar's artistic success over this span was extraordinary. Their first 10 films had an average Rotten Tomatoes score of 94%, with only *Cars* coming in below 90%. Eight Pixar films have been awarded an Academy Award for Best Animated Feature, and two of their films have been nominated for Best Picture, an impressive achievement for an animated film.

Their commercial success has been no less impressive. As the chart below illustrates, on average these films achieved a gross profitability nearly four times that of the average of all other theatrical releases or all non-Pixar animated films.

Figure 6.2: US Gross Profit Margin of Theatrical Release Movies (1980–2008)[56]

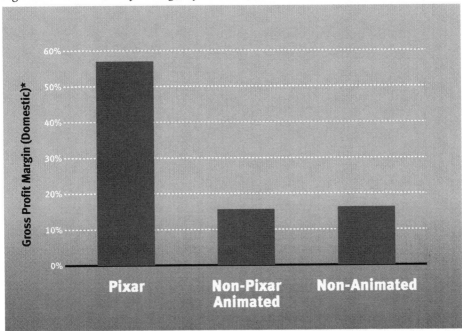

*(US Box Office – Production Costs)/(Production Costs)

Together their worldwide gross stands at $5.3B, which does not include substantial merchandise sales and bolstered theme park profits.

This aggregate performance is impressive but equally impressive is the film-by-film performance. Every film had a positive gross profit margin and all but *WALL-E* exceeded industry averages.[57] This astonishing success emerged from a company that had shrunk to less than 50 employees by 1990 and that had frequently teetered on ruin, often sustained only by Steve Jobs' largesse.

Figure 6.3: Gross Profit Margin of Pixar Films vs. Industry Averages (1980–2008)

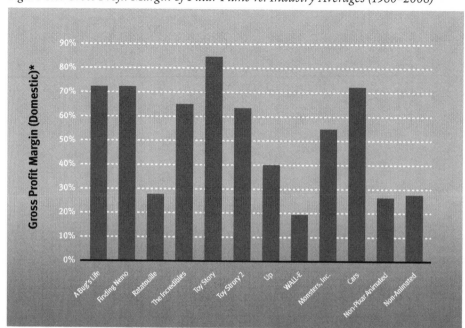

*(US Box Office – Production Costs)/(Production Costs)

The Brain Trust

There is no precedent for this sort of sustained success in the movie business. Certain directors—William Wyler and Stephen Spielberg, for example—or certain franchise series—*Indiana Jones* and the *Rocky* movies, to name a couple—have impressive multiple commercial successes, but no one can boast such a long and unbroken track record, involving multiple directors and teams.

There could be nothing more strategic in every sense of the word. Pixar's superior performance and market cap duly translated into shareholder value, with a $7.4B final value at the time of Disney's acquisition in 2006. It was this transaction, not his earnings at Apple, that accounted for most of Steve Jobs' net worth. Without question—Pixar was wielding some sort of Power.

But the question is: "What type of Power?" Pixar doesn't seem to fit the mold of the Power types I have discussed so far. Movies are a collaborative creative endeavor; as such, they are usually immune to the predictable recurrent triumphs indicative of Power. But at Pixar, some Factor X enabled them to beat the long odds. To fathom this hidden factor, we must probe the Pixar backstory.

In February of 1986, George Lucas, financially stressed by his 1983 divorce settlement, spun out The Graphics Group of the Computer Division of Lucasfilm to Steve Jobs for $5M. The newly independent company was renamed the Pixar Computer Group, and it brought under one roof three extraordinary people:

- John Lasseter: an animation genius who had only two years before been fired by Disney for his tireless advocacy for CGI in animation.

- Ed Catmull: a pioneer CGI computer scientist who possessed the intelligence, self-confidence and humanity to master the nearly impossible art of managing high-octane creatives.

- Steve Jobs: the brilliant and temperamental entrepreneur, who was then struggling with Next Computer, having, only two years prior, been unceremoniously ousted from Apple Computer in a power struggle with John Sculley.

Great businesses are often blessed with one founding genius. Pixar had three: Jobs became Chairman of the Board and the majority shareholder, Catmull became President and Lasseter became head of their animation department. Exclude any one of this trio, and the Pixar fable would have had an unhappy ending.

Of course, tri-partite leadership is challenging in the best of cases, but it worked at Pixar. As Pixar filmmaker Pete Docter told me:

> "Here there was a clear definition of power: John on creative, Ed on technical, and Jobs on business and financial. There was an implicit trust of each other, as well as one guy with the final word (Steve)."[58]

But even with these three engaged and committed, Pixar still struggled to survive its early years, draining cash and taxing Jobs' net worth. The company was initially focused on selling specialized hardware—but only as a survival tactic.

At the same time, it was building up its animation department with key CalArts hires: Andrew Stanton and Pete Docter.

After deep layoffs terminated Pixar's hardware aspirations, a three-picture deal with its computer customer, Disney, gave Pixar a new lease on life in 1991. Surely it was Jobs' "reality distortion field" that made this possible—a nearly bankrupt pipsqueak landing The Walt Disney Company as a filmmaking partner.

The gestation and birth of *Toy Story* was itself a "Perils of Pauline" roller coaster ride. There were false starts, conflicts, do-or-die deadlines, politics and epiphanies. And many, many late nights. Like a Marines squad that has gone to war and back, the filmmaking team forged deep, resilient bonds of trust, respect and understanding. The next two films extended and strengthened them.

This "Band of Brothers" later came to form the core of the group known as the Brain Trust, the creative cadre instrumental to the studio's sustained success. This core group is the Factor X that lies at the heart of Pixar's Power.

Cornered Resource: the Benefit and the Barrier

This Power type is given a name in Economics: Cornered Resource. The services of this cohesive group of talented, battle-hardened veterans were available only to Pixar; they had it cornered. To put this into our 7 Powers framework:

> *Benefit.* In the Pixar case, this resource produced an uncommonly appealing product—"superior deliverables"—driving demand with very attractive price/volume combinations in the form of huge box office returns. No doubt—this was material (a large $\overline{m}$ in the Fundamental Equation of Strategy). In other instances, however, the Cornered Resource can emerge in varied forms, offering uniquely different benefits. It might, for example, be preferential access to a valuable patent, such as that for a blockbuster drug; a required input, such as a cement producer's ownership of a nearby limestone source, or a cost-saving production manufacturing

approach, such as Bausch and Lomb's spin casting technology for soft contact lenses.

Barrier. The Barrier in Cornered Resource is unlike anything we have encountered before. You might wonder: "Why does Pixar retain the Brain Trust?" Any one of this group would be highly sought after by other animated film companies, and yet over this period, and no doubt into the future, they have stayed with Pixar. Even during the company's rocky beginning, there was a loyalty that went beyond simple financial calculation. To illustrate: in 1988, long before Disney began its association with Pixar, Lasseter won an Academy Award for his Pixar short *Tin Toy,* prompting Disney CEO Michael Eisner and Disney Chairman Jeffrey Katzenberg to try to recruit their former employee back into the Disney fold. Lasseter demurred: "I can go to Disney and be a director, or I can stay here and make history."[59] So in Pixar's case, the Barrier was personal choice. In the case of spin casting technology, it is patent law, and in the case of cement inputs, it is property rights. Our general term for this sort of barrier is "fiat"; it is not based on ongoing interaction but rather comes by decree, either general or personal. In a case of the cart driving the donkey, it was Lasseter's commitment to Pixar that helped convince Katzenberg to do the three-picture deal with Pixar in 1991. Likewise, Disney's later CEO, Bob Iger, would decide to acquire Pixar only after realizing such an acquisition would be the sole means of bringing Pixar's talent to Disney's flagging animation group. The subsequent revival of Disney Animation affirmed his wisdom.

This now allows me to place Cornered Resource on our 7 Powers display.

Figure 6.4: Cornered Resource in the 7 Powers

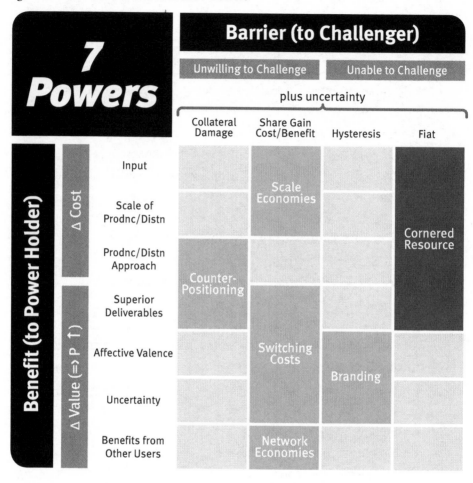

Cornered Resource definition:

Preferential access at attractive terms to a coveted asset that can independently enhance value.

The Five Tests of a Cornered Resource

The Power hurdle is high: to qualify, an attribute must be sufficiently potent to drive high-potential, persistent differential margins ($\overline{m} \gg 0$), with operational excellence spanning the gap between potential and actual. With an enterprise like Pixar, there are numerous resources critical to success, and sorting through this multiplicy to try to isolate the Power source can be a challenge. Over the years I have found that five screening tests for a Cornered Resource often help in this process.

1. *Idiosyncratic.* If a firm repeatedly acquires coveted assets at attractive terms, then the proper strategy question is, "Why are they able to do this?" For example, if one discovered that Exxon was able to persistently gain the rights to desirable hydrocarbon properties, then understanding their path to access would be the more crux issue. Perhaps their relative scale allows them to develop better discovery processes? If so, their discovery processes are the Cornered Resource, the true source of Power, and it would be misleading to simply cite only the acquired leases.

Figure 6.5: Early Pixar Film Directors

Movie	Year	Director	Original Toy Story Team?
Toy Story	1995	John Lasseter	
A Bug's Life	1998	John Lasseter	
Toy Story 2	1999	John Lasseter	
Monsters, Inc.	2001	Pete Docter	
Finding Nemo	2003	Andrew Stanton	
The Incredibles	2004	Brad Bird	
Cars	2006	John Lasseter	
Ratatouille	2007	Brad Bird	
WALL-E	2008	Andrew Stanton	
Up	2009	Pete Docter	
Toy Story 3	2010	Lee Unkrich	

Examining the Pixar Brain Trust through this lens, then, proves highly informative. In particular, you might notice one striking aspect of the Brain Trust: it is largely restricted to a specific set of individuals. As a first indication, consider that every one of their first eleven films was directed by one of this group (except for Brad Bird, discussed below).

Further, Pixar's record shows that simple inclusion into the group will not preternaturally endow newbie directors with the "Brain Trust process." Such directors frequently fail, as evidenced by the replacement of Ash and Colin Brady on *Toy Story 2,* Jan Pinkava on *Ratatouille* and Brenda Chapman on *Brave.*

I believe the Brain Trust is more than a combination of individual talents; rather it is the foundational members' shared experience in the early trial years that has yielded one success after another. If, indeed, we observed new directors being brought into the fold and achieving Pixar-level commercial and artistic success, then we could conclude that Power came not from the Brain Trust but instead from some deeper current. From this assessment, I have come to believe that the most important strategic challenge for Pixar is renewal of its director pool. An informed observer might ask about Brad Bird, who masterminded several of Pixar's biggest successes, coming into the studio and directing *The Incredibles* based on a screenplay he had previously developed outside the purview of the Brain Trust, and later stepping in to rescue *Ratatouille.* Wouldn't he exemplify the sort of untested "outsider" director mentioned above? In fact, not really. On closer inspection, Brad Bird fits the assessment of the restricted nature of the Brain Trust. A classmate and friend of Lasseter from CalArts, Bird already shared a creative shorthand with many of the central figures of the Brain Trust. More, he was an accomplished and established animated film director upon his arrival at Pixar, as demonstrated by his fine film *The Iron Giant.*[60]

2. *Non-arbitraged.* What if a firm gains preferential access to a coveted resource, but then pays a price that fully arbitrages out the rents attributable to this resource? In this case, it fails the differential return test of Power. Consider movie stars. A turn by Brad Pitt would probably advance box office prospects, therefore proving "coveted," but his compensation

captures much or all of this additional value and so fails the Power test. Likewise, although the Pixar Brain Trust is highly compensated, the amounts do not come close to matching their value. I was an investor in Pixar when it was public, and I realized a very nice return over the life of my investment, until the Disney acquisition.

3. *Transferable.* If a resource creates value at a single company but would fail to do so at other companies, then isolating that resource as the source of Power would entail overlooking some other essential complement beyond operational excellence. The word "coveted" in the definition conveys the expectation by many that the asset will create value. In the lead-up to his acquisition of Pixar, Bob Iger had an epiphany: the legacy of Disney's animated characters formed the core of the corporation, and only the Pixar team could revive that legacy. This motivated his purchase of Pixar, as well as his decision to place Catmull and Lasseter at the helm of Disney Animation, which resulted in the meteoric revival of that storied division. Such a comeback would never have been possible without Catmull and Lasseter in key decision-making roles, and the Brain Trust on call, and it ultimately vindicated the steep price paid by Disney. This resource was transferable.

4. *Ongoing.* In searching for Power, a strategist tries to isolate a causal factor that explains continued differential returns. There's a contrapositive to this, too: one would then expect differential returns to suffer should the identified factor be taken away. Clearly this perspective has bearing on the identification of a Cornered Resource. There may be many factors that proved formative in developing Power but whose contributions then became embedded in the business.

For example, Post-it notes emerged as a highly profitable business for 3M only because Dr. Spenser Silver tirelessly sought commercial application for his not-so-sticky glue. Once the Post-It application was established, the business' differential returns were not predicated on him and his unique glue, but rather a different—in part, at least—Cornered Resource:

U.S. Patent 3,691,140. U.S. Patent 5,194,299 and the Post-It Trademark. At Pixar, Steve Jobs offered a similar case in point. He was essential to Pixar's ascendancy—viewing him simply as patient money utterly understates his contribution—but his importance diminished as Pixar developed, and eventually his value became embedded in the company to the point where his continued presence was no longer needed to drive differential returns. The Brain Trust, on the other hand, endures as the sustaining force behind their success.

5. *Sufficient.* The final Cornered Resource test concerns completeness: for a resource to qualify as Power, it must be sufficient for continued differential returns, assuming operational excellence.

Frequently, as I have observed, many will mistake specific leadership for a Cornered Resource; in fact, it fails this sufficiency test. For example, I am a fan of the abilities of George Fisher. He did a fine job leading Motorola. When he took the helm at Kodak, there were high hopes that his presence would lead to a revival of the company—i.e. that he was a Cornered Resource. The rough patch that followed was, in my view, not his fault; it was merely an indication of the hopeless cul-de-sac created by the company's focus on chemical film in a solid-state age. These difficulties, however, yield an insight: Fisher was not a Cornered Resource, and the Motorola success involved other complements to his talent that were not later present at Kodak.

Another way to put this is that a Cornered Resource is a *sufficient* condition for potential for differential returns. In my view, current evidence best supports the assertion that the Pixar Brain Trust as a unit is the company's Cornered Resource, as opposed to individual members, such as Catmull or Lasseter. One might view Lasseter + Catmull together as the real Cornered Resource and then suggest that the other Brain Trust hires serve merely as a reflection of their selection skills. You could even view the revival of Disney Animation under Lasseter's and Catmull's leadership as evidentiary to this view. The failure of newbie Pixar directors, however, tends to belie this.

Figure 6.6: Power Intensity Determinants

	Industry Economics	**Competitive Position**
Scale Economies	Scale economy intensity	Relative scale
Network Economies	Network effect intensity	Absolute difference in installed base
Counter-Positioning	New business model superiority + collateral damage to old	Binary: entrant—new model; incumbent—old model
Switching Costs	Magnitude (intensity) of switching costs	Number of current customers
Branding	Time constant and potential magnitude of Branding effect	Duration of brand investing
Cornered Resource	Price &/or cost increment due to CR	Preferred access at a non-arbitraging price

Appendix 6.1: the Resource Based View

The notion of resource is a broad and inclusive one that goes far beyond the considerations of this chapter. There is a major school of thought in Strategy, the Resource Based View ("RBV"), which focuses on resources. I have benefited from the fine scholarship of the RBV and even had the privilege of studying studying under the brilliant Professor Richard R. Nelson, one of the RBV pioneers.

Businesses encompass not just products and services, but the abilities that enable their efficient production. There are immediate abilities, specific to current output, and higher-level abilities, which circumscribe the company's domains of competitiveness. There are even further stages beyond these which shape the ways in which these higher-level abilities may transform over time. Core competencies, distinctive competencies, routines, capabilities and dynamic capabilities all figure into this conversation.

I have intentionally restricted this chapter's treatment of resources. First, my treatment narrows the topic by looking only at resources which qualify as Power. The tests above are meant to help the practitioner eliminate resources that may well be notable but are not strategic in the sense that I use the term.

Secondly, though, a more profound narrowing: this part of my book is restricted to statics of Power. The RBV figures more heavily into dynamics. When I move on to that topic in Part II, we will observe that invention is the first cause of Power. There, in exploring the endogenous determinants of invention, the concept of resources, in the broader sense used by the RBV, will feature more prominently.

Appendix 6.2: Surplus Leader Margin for Cornered Resource

To calibrate the intensity of Power, I ask the question "What governs profitability of the company with Power (S) when prices are such that the company with no Power (W) makes no profit at all?"

Suppose the Cornered Resource (CR) possessed by S results in superior deliverables. This, for example, fits the Pixar case of consistently compelling movies.

We further suppose that S realizes a per unit increase in profits from this resource of Δ. This could come from a price increase due to superior deliverables or a cost decrease. (In the Pixar case, the superior deliverables are more focused on getting higher volumes, theater attendance. One way to think about this: the Δ that would result if pricing were such that only average volumes resulted).

Also for simplicity, assume that there are no fixed costs to production.

$$\text{Profit} \equiv \pi = [P - c + \Delta]\, Q \quad \text{with} \quad P \equiv \text{price}$$
$$c \equiv \text{variable cost per unit}$$
$$Q \equiv \text{units produced per time period}$$

Also suppose that the incremental cost of the CR is the fixed amount per year k. In the Pixar case this would be the extra annual compensation that would be paid to the discussed core group *above* what would be paid, if individuals with similar training were hired to replace them.

So   S' profit $\equiv {}_S\pi = [{}_WP + \Delta - c]\, {}_SQ - k$

For the Surplus Leader Margin (SLM) we assess:

What governs S's margins if P is set ∋ ${}_W\pi = 0$?

${}_W\pi = 0 \Rightarrow \qquad 0 = ({}_WP - c)\, {}_SQ \Rightarrow {}_WP = c$

S has an additional profit from the CR: Δ

S also incurs an additional fixed cost of k (k need not be positive)

So ${}_S\pi = [(\Delta + {}_WP) - c]\, {}_SQ - k$ substituting ${}_WP = c$

${}_S\pi = \Delta\, {}_SQ - k$ dividing by revenues $[(\Delta + {}_WP)^*{}_SQ]$ results in margin

So $\quad _s\text{margin} = \Delta \, _sQ/(\Delta + _wP)^*_sQ - k/(\Delta + _wP)^*_sQ$

$$\boxed{\text{SLM} = \Delta/(\Delta + _wP) - k/(\Delta + _wP)^*_sQ}$$

= [Margin increase due to CR] – [CR cost per dollar sales]

Industry economics: Δ, k

Competitive position: control of CR by fiat or not

CHAPTER 7
PROCESS POWER
STEP BY STEP

You have now reviewed six of the 7 Powers. This chapter will complete your tour by discussing the final type, Process Power. I save it until last because it is rare. I will use the Toyota Motor Corporation as a case.

By the time I graduated from college in 1969, a close friend and fellow Vermont motorhead had already acquired the Toyota dealership rights for our area in Northern New England. It seemed a risky move at the time, but he considered it an investment in an extraordinary upstart. Toyota's boxy new Corolla had none of the performance chops that usually attracted the attention and affection of our group. Instead, what impressed my friend was the sheer quality of their automobiles, which was such a contrast to those offered by the world-leading Detroit behemoths.

Back then, Toyota hardly blipped on anyone's radar in the US auto market: they held a .1% market share compared to General Motors' astounding 48.5%. Even so, my friend's investment was prescient—Toyota's meager presence belied a deeper reality. They had already spent nearly two decades relentlessly honing a fearsome competitive asset: the Toyota Production System (TPS).

In 1950 Eiji Toyoda, then a managing director of Toyota Motor Company, spent three months in Dearborn, Michigan studying the Ford River Rouge Plant, "the largest integrated factory in the world."[61] His earlier visit to Ford in 1929 had left him profoundly impressed by the Ford revolution in manufacturing. His reaction to the 1950 visit was quite the opposite. The Ford plant maintained deep inventories, which were used to smooth out production irregularities, but this seemed wasteful to Toyoda-san. He was more impressed by the supermarkets he saw around the city: their system of restocking only when shelves had gone empty aligned with the parsimonious nature he had developed over years of war-driven shortages. He thought he could do better than Ford, and so he set to work.[62]

But developing a superior automobile manufacturing process was no fool's errand. Even the Ford Model T, a poster child for simplicity in the car business, had 7,882 assembly steps.[63] And assembly formed only a piece of the puzzle—a vast supply chain reached backwards, mirrored in its complexity by the geographically dispersed dealership distribution system that lay downstream from the point of assembly.

But the impulse for quality and efficiency had deep roots in Toyota, stretching all the way back to Sakichi Toyoda's 1890 invention of the Toyoda Wooden Hand Loom. So bit-by-bit, in the wake of the 1950 Ford visit, Toyota developed what would later be called the TPS. The resulting unsurpassed quality and durability of their cars met a welcome audience, many of whom were exhausted with their fragile American models and a Detroit mentality predicated on the notion of planned obsolescence, or "dynamic obsolescence" as GM's Alfred Sloan dubbed it.[64] The outcome was stunning, as seen by the chart below.

Figure 7.1: Shares in US Automobile Market[65]

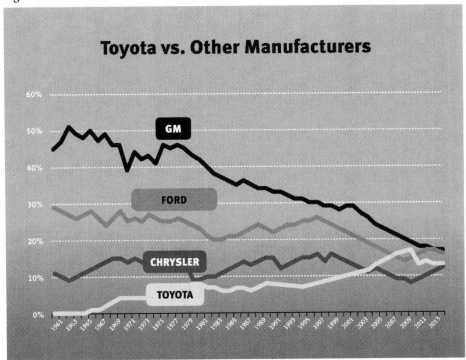

From out of nowhere, by 2014 Toyota managed to pull nearly even with GM and Ford in the U.S. market. Over the same period, GM collapsed: its U.S. share plummeting from half the U.S. market to less than 20%. Worldwide, Toyota's market share trends were even more impressive.

The persistence of these shifts, over decades, is as notable as their magnitude. Already by 1980, the handwriting was on the wall: Toyota was soaking up market share and GM was in decline. In the 1960s GM had been looked upon as one of the best-run companies in the world, and this slow-motion collapse left the company considering whether they ought to take a page from their competitor's playbook. And so in 1984 GM established NUMMI, a joint venture with Toyota, which would utilize Toyota production techniques to produce compact cars at a Fremont, California plant. GM accepted Toyota as the expert here, and the Fremont workers were sent to Japan for training.

The joint venture got off to a fast start, and the low defect rates of NUMMI cars quickly approached those of Toyota in their Japanese facilities. GM had high hopes that the lessons learned from this endeavor would be readily transferable to their numerous other plants around the world.

But it was not to be. Although Toyota offered full transparency regarding NUMMI practices, GM just couldn't replicate the NUMMI results in its own facilities. This was not merely incompetence—the inability to mimic the TPS was shared by many, as noted in a *Harvard Business Review* article:

> "What's curious is that few manufacturers have managed to imitate Toyota successfully even though the company has been extraordinarily open about its practices. Hundreds of thousands of executives from thousands of businesses have toured Toyota's plants in Japan and the United States."[66]

This failure to transfer the NUMMI practices perpetuated the trend noted before: GM's inexorable decline continued for decades, despite the success of NUMMI.

So what was the underlying challenge? GM was motivated, willing and able to spend, and, with NUMMI, seemingly well positioned to acquire the needed knowledge.

Here's the rub: the TPS is not what it seems. On the surface, it consists of a fairly straightforward variety of interlocking procedures, such as just-in-time production, *kaizen* (continuous improvement), *kanban* (inventory control), *andon* cords (devices to allow workers to stop production and identify a problem so it can be fixed). Observing all this, GM workers naturally assumed you could clone TPS by copying these procedures.

It turns out, though, that these production techniques merely manifest some deeper, more complex system, as illustrated by the frustration of Ernie Shaefer, the manager of the GM plant in Van Nuys, California:

> "…what's different when you walk into the NUMMI plant? Well, you can see a lot of things different. But the one thing you don't see is the system that supports the NUMMI plant. I don't think, at that time, anybody understood the large nature of this system…. You know, they never prohibited us from walking through the plant, understanding, even asking questions of some of their key people. I've often puzzled over that—why they did that. And I think they recognized, we were asking all the wrong questions. We didn't understand this bigger picture thing. All of our questions were focused on the floor, the assembly plant, what's happening on the line. That's not the real issue. The issue is how do you support that system with all the other functions that have to take place in the organization?"[67]

So despite best intentions, and many millions of investment dollars, achieving Toyota-like outcomes proved an elusive medium-term goal for GM. Apparently there existed a Barrier of some sort. Combine this with the twin Benefits of cost efficiency and dramatic quality improvements and there remains only one conclusion—Toyota had tapped some elusive source of Power. Their rising share price throughout these decades, graphed below and resulting in a company worth nearly $200B, serves as final indicator. But what type of Power were they wielding?

Toyota Stock Price

Process Power

The TPS exemplifies a rare Power type: Process Power. Let me characterize Process Power more formally using the usual Benefit and Barriers dimensions of the 7 Powers framework.

Benefit. A company with Process Power is able to improve product attributes and/or lower costs as a result of process improvements embedded within the organization. For example, Toyota has maintained the quality increases and cost reductions of the TPS over a span of decades; these assets do not disappear as new workers are brought in and older workers retire.

Barrier. The Barrier in Process Power is hysteresis: these process advances are difficult to replicate, and can only be achieved over a long time period of sustained evolutionary advance. This inherent speed limit in achieving the Benefit results from two factors:

1. *Complexity.* Returning to our example: automobile production, combined with all the logistic chains which support it, entails enormous complexity. If process improvements touch many parts of these chains, as they did with Toyota, then achieving them quickly will prove challenging, if not impossible.

2. *Opacity.* The development of TPS should tip us off to the long time constant inevitably faced by would-be imitators. The system was fashioned from the bottom up, over decades of trial and error. The fundamental tenets were never formally codified, and much of the organizational knowledge remained tacit, rather than explicit. It would not be an exaggeration to say that even Toyota did not have a full, top-down understanding of what they had created—it took fully fifteen years, for instance, before they were able to transfer TPS to their suppliers. GM's experience with NUMMI also implies the tacit character of this knowledge: even when Toyota wanted to illuminate their work processes, they could not entirely do so.

This Benefit/Barrier combination allows us to place Process Power on the 7 Powers chart.

Figure 7.3: Process Power in the 7 Powers

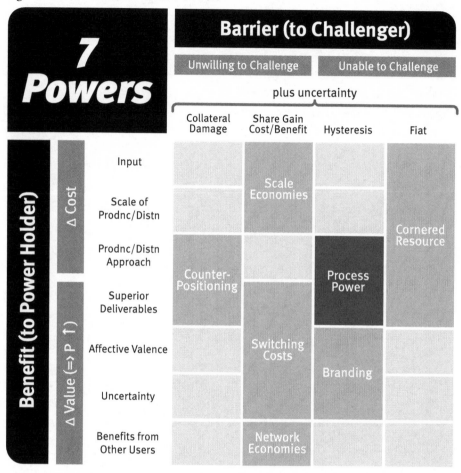

Which brings us to our definition of Process Power:

> *Embedded company organization and activity sets which enable lower costs and/or superior product, and which can be matched only by an extended commitment.*

Process Power and the Discipline of Strategy

Process Power has important intersections with the evolution of the discipline of Strategy.[69] By characterizing these, we can better understand the nature of Process Power and why it is so rare.

Strategy versus Operational Excellence. Professor Michael Porter of Harvard created quite a stir with his long-ago insistence that operational excellence is not strategy.[70] His reason for doing so, however, completely aligns with the "No Arbitrage" assumption of this book: improvements that can be readily mimicked are not strategic, because they do not contribute to increasing $\bar{m}$ or $\bar{s}$ in the Fundamental Equation of Strategy, as these are long-term equilibrium values.

But wait a minute. Aren't the step-by-step improvements that drive Process Power exactly what much operational excellence is all about? Yes, they are, but this represents only the Benefit side, which brings us to an important point of caution about Process Power. The type of Benefit it cites—evolutionary bottom-up improvement—stands at the heart of operational excellence; as such, it is quite common. The rarity of Process Power results from the infrequency of the Barrier: an unyielding, long-time constant for the improvements in question. No matter how much you invest or how hard you try, the desired improvements are constrained by a boundary of potential that is tied to time, as seen in the NUMMI experience of GM.

Perhaps the best way to think of it is this: Process Power equals operational excellence, plus hysteresis. Having said that, such hysteresis occurs so rarely that I am in strong agreement with Professor Porter's sentiments.[71]

If one were to adopt a different definition of Strategy—something like "everything that is important"—then operational excellence would be strategic. As is, though, operational excellence—while important, hard to achieve and worthy of management mind share—is not sufficient to gain competitive advantage. Professor Porter would not dispute this.

The Experience Curve. A concept known as "The Experience Curve" loomed large in the formative years of the Boston Consulting Group and Bain & Company's strategy practices. The Experience Curve was based on the empirical observation that many company costs seem to follow a downward trajectory that falls within a specified envelope: for each doubling of units produced (what's meant formally by "experience"), the deflated cost per unit would be between 70% and 85% of what it had previously been prior to the doubling (referred to as "Slope").

This view is not naïve, as indicated by the histogram derived from data in a 1990 *Science* article:[72]

Figure 7.4: Experience Curve Sample

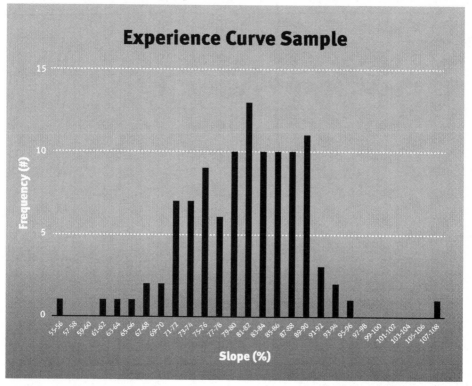

In this sample, about 60% of their 108 examples exhibited slopes in the 70–85% range.

You might be tempted to read these data as disproving my assertion that Process Power is uncommon; rather, you might say, it is a usual business condition driven by "experience." Unfortunately, these data simply underline the frequency of the benefits attending operational excellence. The improvements mapped above refer only to gains made *over time*; they tell us nothing about the relative position of multiple firms *at a single point in time*. For example, based on the Experience Curve, there would be no cost differences *at any point in time* between firms of different sizes but all firms realizing similar year-to-year gains.[73]

Let's use a simple thought experiment to clarify my assertion that the gains over time indicated by the Experience Curve are widely shared amongst firms. If the relationship between experience held across all firms at a single point in time, then one would commonly expect a firm with a 2x size advantage over its largest competitor to sustain operating margin gains of 15% to 30%. The rarity of such huge differences underscores an irony: the Experience Curve does not suggest Power, but rather it indirectly testifies to Professor Porter's point—the ubiquity of competitive arbitrage.

Routine. As mentioned before, while in graduate school I had the privilege of studying under Professor Richard R. Nelson. Dick is a fearlessly original thinker, and Strategy was one of the many areas to which he made seminal contributions. His book, *An Evolutionary Theory of Economic Change*, written with Sydney Winter, put forth the view that innovation was rarely driven by top-down purposive initiatives, but rather by the adaptive responses of "boundedly rational"[74] agents. Such evolutionary innovation manifests, often tacitly, in new processes that they dubbed "routines." This view maps well to what we saw with the TPS.

Nelson and Winter's book is often considered foundational to the aforementioned Resource Based View of Strategy. In Economic History, there is a notion called the "colligation problem": how far back should you go in understanding causation?[75] The RBV perspective holds that if you stop at competitive advantage, you inappropriately truncate your investigation. Rather, you might gain deeper insight by considering what more fundamental prior dispositions ("resources") enabled the development of competitive positions in the first place. The well-disseminated notion of Core Competencies[76] is one expression of this view.

Professors Nelson and Winter's idea of routines provides an excellent launch pad for such inquiries. But usually such routines represent a Benefit with no Barrier; hence they do not result in Power. You might ask, then, is the RBV more revealing for operational excellence than for Strategy? This is not my view. Rich Strategy characterizations result from the RBV, but they have more to do with Dynamics, the subject of the second part of this book. Indeed, as we will see in

Part II, operational excellence in general carries profound import in establishing certain types of Power.

With this seventh Power type I am now able to finish the Competitive Position/Industry Economics roll-up that I began in Chapter 1.

Figure 7.5: Power Intensity Determinants

	Industry Economics	**Competitive Position**
Scale Economies	Scale economy intensity	Relative scale
Network Economies	Network effect intensity	Absolute difference in installed base
Counter-Positioning	New business model superiority + collateral damage to old	Binary: entrant—new model; incumbent—old model
Switching Costs	Magnitude (intensity) of switching costs	Number of current customers
Branding	Time constant and potential magnitude of Branding effect	Duration of brand investing
Cornered Resources	Price &/or cost increment due to CR	Preferred access at a non-arbitraging price
Process Power	Time constant and potential magnitude of Process Power effect	Relative duration of Process Power advances

7 Powers Wrap-Up

You are there. My goal has been all along to provide you with a strategy compass to guide you as you move forward with your business. In the Introduction I noted that to fulfill this function the 7 Powers would have to clear the high hurdle of "simple but not simplistic." Early on, I explicitly tied my concepts back to value with the Fundamental Equation of Strategy. This gave us confidence that what followed was not simplistic. With this chapter, I have now completed the 7 Powers. I am confident from interacting with many businesspeople that this is sufficiently simple to be such a compass. I trust you will find it so as well.

Figure 7.6: The 7 Powers

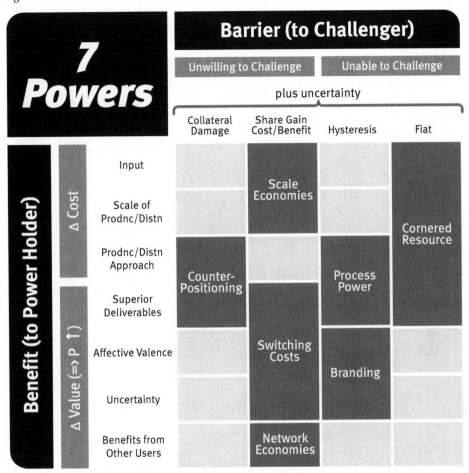

We will now move on to Part II of this book and engage the issue of Dynamics: "How are these seven Power types developed?"

Appendix 7.1: Process Power Surplus Leader Margin

To calibrate the intensity of Power, I ask the question "What governs the leader's profitability of the company with Power (S) when prices are such that the company with no Power (W) makes no profit at all?"

In the case of Process Power, I assume all costs are marginal, so the zero-challenger profit price equals marginal costs. I focus on the case where the leader costs are lower due to its Process Power (alternately, it might charge a higher price due to its Process Power, or both). As a consequence:

$$\text{Profit} \equiv \pi = [P - c]\, Q$$

$$\text{with} \quad P \equiv \text{price}$$
$$c \equiv \text{marginal cost per unit}$$
$$Q \equiv \text{units produced per time period}$$

To determine SLM, assess:

What are S's margins if P is set $\ni {}^W\pi = 0$?

$${}^W\pi = 0 \Rightarrow \qquad 0 = (P - {}^Wc)\, {}^SQ \qquad \Rightarrow P = {}^Wc$$

Suppose:

$$D\,(t) \equiv \text{W's cost multiple at time t}$$
$$Z \equiv \text{maximum potential cost multiple}$$
$$F \equiv \text{cycle time compression factor}$$

^Wc are a multiple of ^Sc, so $^Wc = D(t) * {}^Sc$

$$\therefore \qquad {}^S\pi = [P - {}^Sc]\, {}^SQ = [D(t) * {}^Sc - {}^Sc]\, {}^SQ$$

$${}^S\pi = (D(t)-1)\, {}^Sc\, {}^SQ$$

$${}^S\text{Margin} = (D(t)-1)\, {}^Sc\, {}^SQ / (\,D(t)\, {}^Sc\, {}^SQ) = 1 - 1/D(t)$$

Or $\quad \boxed{\textbf{SLM} = \textbf{1} - \textbf{1/D(t)}} \quad$ with $D(t) = Z/(1 + (Z-1)e^{-Ft})$

Industry economics define the function $D()$, which determines the potential magnitude and sustainability of leverage. $D(t)$ is an increasing function of t, reflecting that Process Power requires action over time to be increased. The logistic function was chosen to reflect the reinforcing aspect of Process Power investment, while allowing diminishing marginal returns over time. The particular form specified above for D(t) ensures that D(t)=1 at t=0 by adjusting the location parameter as a function of F and Z. When F is larger, the logistic curve is steeper and the Process Power cycle time is shorter. When F is smaller, the logistic curve is shallower and the Process Power cycle time is longer.

Time t represents the competitive position that S has relative to W in developing Process Power, because it determines the ability of a competitor starting at time t = 0 to catch up to the strong firm at time t=t. Z and F (i.e., D[t]) determine industry position. As can be seen in Figure 7.6, the longer the life cycle, the farther behind the weak competitor, and so the harder it is to catch up to the strong firm. The sustainability of the process depends on the shape of the D(t) function relative to D(0) for all t in the case of the weakest competitor with no Process Power, and an alternative D'(t) function (i.e., an alternative F') and alternative t for another competitor.

Figure 7.6: Process Power as a Function of Time

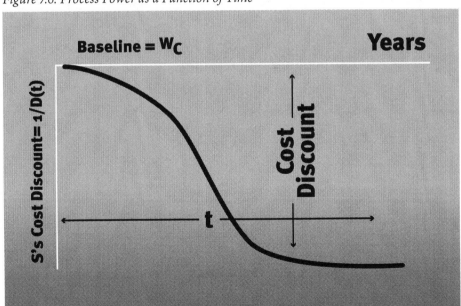

PART II
STRATEGY DYNAMICS

CHAPTER 8
THE PATH TO POWER
"ME TOO" WON'T DO

We have come a long way together on our journey to enable you to flexibly develop your company strategy. Each of the prior seven chapters detailed one Power type, and block by block I have constructed the 7 Powers. You now possess a potent strategy compass: it covers all attractive strategic positions for all businesses in all locations.[77] Armed with one or more of these Power types, your business is ideally positioned to become a durable cash-generator, despite the best efforts of competitors. If you possess none of these, your business is at risk. Period.

The contribution of the 7 Powers does not stop there, however. You still need a guide for your journey, a roadmap for the creation of Power. You might anticipate the various routes being so idiosyncratic as to preclude meaningful generalization. But the 7 Powers enables us to penetrate through this tangle of details to the deeper core.

By now you know that your business must achieve Power, or else face ruin. So you are probably asking yourself two questions: "*What* must I do to establish Power?" and "*When* can I establish it?" Part II of this book reveals the answers to these questions. The question of "What?" serves as the subject of this chapter, and "When?" the subject of the next.

I will start with a single case: Netflix's streaming business. From there, I will generalize on the "How?" question for all businesses. But let me offer a first insight right here up front: all Power starts with invention. Once we have explored this notion, I will then move on to the ways in which invention propels the other key element of the Fundamental Equation of Strategy—market size.

Out of the Frying Pan...

When I became an investor in Netflix in 2003, my investment hypothesis had two legs:

1. Netflix's DVD-rental business had Power: Counter-Positioning to the brick-and-mortar incumbent, Blockbuster; Process Power, as well as modest spatial distribution Scale Economies relative to other DVD-by-mail wannabes.

2. This Power was not properly recognized by the investment community.

My hypothesis proved correct, as Netflix handily beat back other like competitors, while also winning a bruising battle against Blockbuster, with a finale as definitive as any strategist could hope for: on September 23, 2010, Blockbuster declared Chapter 11 bankruptcy. The dramatic demise of this previously high-flying competitor served as testimony to the potency of the Counter-Positioning I had hypothesized.

One might hope that such a victory would have provided a durable sinecure, but that was not in the cards for Netflix, at least not yet. My investment hypothesis carried a two-part caveat. First, I knew DVD rentals were transitory, destined to be supplanted by digital distribution over the Internet.

This was hardly news to Netflix management. Reed Hastings, their CEO and founder, wrote in 2005:

> DVDs will continue to generate big profits in the near future. Netflix has at least another decade of dominance ahead of it. But movies over the Internet are coming, and at some point it will become big business.... That's why the company is called Netflix, not DVD-By-Mail.[78]

The second part of my caveat was likewise cautionary: Netflix had no yet-evident sources of Power in this new modality—the technology to stream was accessible to many, and the powerful content owners were implacably committed to wringing every penny from their rights. I suspect Netflix management might have agreed with me on this assumption too.

The Netflix response to these predicaments? They tested the waters, investing 1–2% of revenue on streaming[79]—not a bet-the-company amount, sure, but hardly trivial. This effort culminated in the launch of the Watch Now feature on January 16, 2007. It was a modest beginning, and the initial offering comprised only about 1000 titles, small compared to their DVD library, which was 100 times larger, but significant still.

Customers responded positively, encouraging Netflix to fuel the fire. The company negotiated in turn with each hardware vendor to achieve device ubiquity; they upped their commitment on content, eventually reaching deals with CBS, Disney, Starz and MTV in 2008–2009, and they constantly refined the backend technology needed to make streaming a seamless customer experience.

By 2010, streaming had become a force for Netflix. At the beginning of 2011, *TechCrunch* headlined "Streaming Is Driving New Subscriber Growth At Netflix,"[80] showing the graph below to document the company's astonishing subscriber growth.

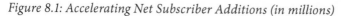
Figure 8.1: Accelerating Net Subscriber Additions (in millions)

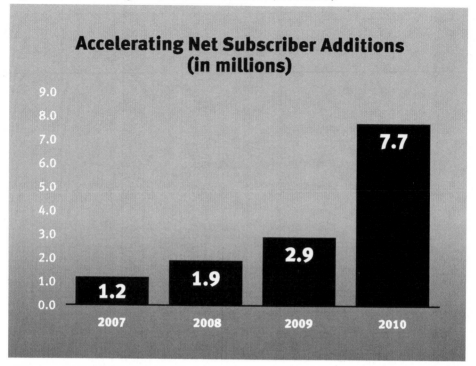

This was good news, but the second part of my caveat still held—streaming had no apparent sources of Power. At last Netflix had come face-to-face with Professor Porter's uncomfortable truth: operational excellence is not strategy.

Yes, operational excellence is essential and constantly challenging; it rightfully occupies the lion's share of management's time. Unfortunately, it does not by itself assure differential margins (a positive $\bar{m}$ in the Fundamental Equation of Strategy) combined with a steady or growing market share ($\bar{s}$ in the FES). Competitors can easily mimic the improvements yielded by operational excellence, eventually arbitraging out the value to the business.

Netflix suffered many acute operational challenges as it moved into streaming, and gradually addressed them. But even these efforts were insufficient to assure continuing differential returns. Consider some examples:

- *User Interface (UI) development.* Netflix rightfully paid a great deal of attention to its UI. The company is a data smart one, and A/B testing of UI alternatives has led to many frequent refinements. Unfortunately, as Blockbuster showed in its mail-order rental competition with Netflix, it is easy to copy a UI.

- *Recommendation engine.* Netflix was a world leader in recommendation engine development, even sponsoring the Netflix Prize, which yielded machine-learning insights still notable in that community. Here one might hypothesize some Scale Economies: as Netflix accumulates more data, the acuity of their recommendations increases. True, but not linear: these advantages paid only diminishing returns, meaning a smaller competitor of an attainable scale could realize most of the same benefit.

- *IT infrastructure.* Video consumes a prodigious amount of bandwidth and storage: by 2011, for example, Netflix had become by far the largest user of peak bandwidth on the Internet. They took the view—perhaps unexpected for a technology company—that this was not their core competence and made the decision (correctly, in my view) to outsource their information technology ("IT"), eventually ending up as a large customer of Amazon Web Services. This relieved many of their IT expansion headaches and allowed them to focus on what they do best.

Each of these areas required relentless and expert focus, and yet solving this multiplicity of problems was not enough. All of the advances could be more or less mimicked by others in the longer term. The potential for Power remained elusive.

Netflix realized that content lay at the heart of the problem. After all, great content ultimately represents any streamer's core value proposition, and for Netflix, it accounted for the bulk of their cost structure. Unfortunately, content holders could "variable cost price" the programming they licensed, charging Netflix according to usage. This put other licensors on an even footing with Netflix, regardless of scale, thus eliminating any chance of Power.

Ted Sarandos, the strategically acute Netflix content head, took the first step in addressing this challenge by pursuing exclusives. At first blush, exclusives seemed a poor choice for Netflix: their higher price meant less content for subscribers. Nevertheless, on August 10, 2010, Netflix and Epix agreed to an exclusive agreement:

> "Adding EPIX to our growing library of streaming content, as the exclusive Internet-only distributor of this great content, marks the continued emergence of Netflix as a leader in entertainment delivered over the Web," said Ted Sarandos.[81]

This changed the game. The price of an exclusive was fixed, which meant some content no longer carried a variable cost. All of a sudden Netflix's substantial scale advantage over other streamers made a difference.

But the owners of potential exclusive properties could take note of Netflix's success. Eventually they would resort to bargaining hard for an outsized share of those returns, even using other streaming competitors as stalking horses. In fact, Epix did exactly this, ending its deal with Netflix and signing up instead with Amazon on Sept 4, 2012.

So again, with Sarandos' approbation, Netflix took the next logical step—originals. Here they took a page out of HBO's playbook—that network's transition to originals had secured their position as a premium cable juggernaut years before. First for Netflix was the modest *Lilyhammer,* but on March 16, 2011, Netflix dropped a bomb. *Deadline Hollywood* splashed:

> *Netflix To Enter Original Programming With Mega Deal For David Fincher-Kevin Spacey Series 'House Of Cards'*[82]

Netflix plunked down $100 million, beating out HBO, CBS and Showtime to lock up twenty-six episodes, two full seasons of the political thriller. It was a big bet, and despite modest assurance from their user stats, a large risk.

They were rewarded with increased subscriptions and numerous awards, including nine Primetime Emmy Nominations, a victory on the Benefit side, but also the beachhead for a victory on the Barrier side. Originals unequivocally rendered content a fixed cost, guaranteeing powerful Scale Economies, and they also permanently altered Netflix's bargaining position with content owners. As Reed Hastings put it:

> "…If the television networks stop selling shows… the company has a game plan. We just do more originals…."[83]

Fast forward to 2015. Originals have now become the centerpiece of Netflix's strategy, as this Wikipedia chart shows.

Figure 8.2: Netflix Originals[84]

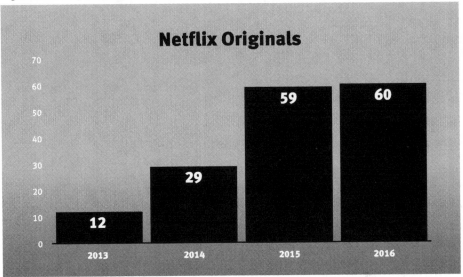

The value created by this robust strategy has been stunning, a nearly 100x gain in share price, culminating in a market cap of about $50B.

Figure 8.3: Netflix Stock Price[85]

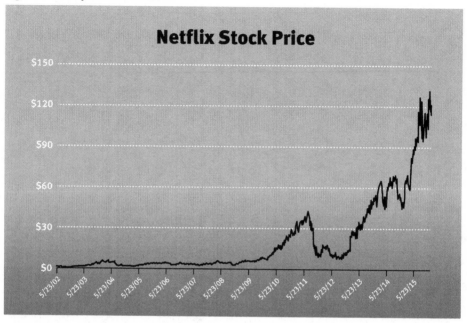

The Rudder Only Works When the Ship Is Moving

Professor Henry Mintzberg's canonical 1987 article[86] rightly characterized such a process as "crafting," rather than designing. The saga of Netflix's ascent exemplifies intelligent adaptation over an extended period in the face of daunting uncertainty. The terrain of entrepreneurs, not planners.

The 100x increase in stock price noted above serves as a signal of the uncertainty that initially existed. Prior to Netflix's success, the value potential was opaque to the investment community, not because investors were thoughtless or ill-informed, but because the "route to Power" was not just unknown, but unknowable—even to Netflix management.

Here's the first important takeaway from our consideration of Dynamics: "getting there" (Dynamics) is completely different from "being there" (Statics). This is a distinction not only for academics but for practitioners as well. For example, in the early days of strategy consulting, the two were frequently conflated: a close study of Statics indicated that high relative market share led to attractive returns; this fed the instinct to gain market share (Dynamics), usually via aggressive pricing.

Such policies usually did not create value, as competitors would push back until the cost of share gains typically outweighed their benefits.

This disconnect might tempt you to reject Statics as a means of understanding Dynamics, but that would be folly. In a prescient article of two decades ago, Professor Porter saw past this error to the underlying premise that inspired my approach:

> A body of theory which links firm characteristics to market outcomes must provide the foundation for any fully dynamic theory of strategy. Otherwise dynamic processes that result in superior performance cannot be discriminated from those that create market positions or company skills that are worthless.[87]

In other words, to assess which journeys are worth taking, you must first understand which destinations are desirable. Fortunately the 7 Powers does exactly that: it maps the only seven worthwhile destinations.

Accordingly, we can look back to my previous discussion of Netflix's streaming saga in Chapter 1, where we viewed it through the lens of Statics. This snaps into focus the crux moves that established the foundations of Power:

1. *Competitive Position: an attractive new service.* Netflix's pioneering rollout excited customers, and their influx propelled Netflix to an early relative scale advantage that the company has never relinquished.

2. *Industry Economics: originals and exclusives.* This converted some content, the largest element of their cost structure, from variable cost to fixed cost, cementing Power by creating Scale Economies for the first time.[88]

These are the profound breakthroughs that forever changed streaming from an unattractive rat race commodity business to a bankable cash flow generator. This is what developing a "route to continuing Power in significant markets" looks like. Again, one is struck by Mintzberg's perspicacity when he dubbed this "crafting." Netflix adaptively found its way to streaming ascendancy via successive thoughtful experimentation, demonstrating once again that action is the first principle of strategy, just as it is in business. This is about as far removed from the orderly analytics of strategic planning as you can imagine.

Invention—the Mother of Power

Okay, that's Netflix and their streaming business. An inspiring tale, no doubt, but one story alone won't cut it. My objective in this chapter is far more ambitious: to help you figure out "What must I do to create Power in my business?"

With Netflix, we saw that creating the streaming business and then segueing to originals propelled their "route to continuing Power in significant markets." With an eye toward deducing a more general understanding, let's take a step back, reexamine all seven types of Power and ask the Dynamics question "What must you do to get there?"

- *Scale Economies.* With this first Power type, you must simultaneously pursue a business model that promises Scale Economies (industry economics), while at the same time offering up a product differentially attractive enough to pull in customers and gain relative share (competitive position).

- *Network Economies.* Here the needs are similar to Scale Economies, except that installed base, rather than sales share, is the goal.

- *Cornered Resource.* You must secure the rights to a valuable resource on attractive terms. This often comes from having developed that resource in the first place and then gaining ownership of it, the most common avenue being a patent award for research developments.

- *Branding.* Over an extensive period of time, you make the consistent creative choices which foster in the customer's mind an affinity that goes beyond the product's objective attributes.

- *Counter-Positioning.* You pioneer a new, superior business model that promises collateral damage for incumbents if mimicked.

- *Switching Costs.* With Switching Costs, you must first attain a customer base, meaning the same new-product requirements demanded of Scale and Network Economies factor in here as well.

- *Process Power.* You evolve a new complex process which renders itself inimitable within a reasonable period and yet offers significant advantages over a longer period of time.

We are covering a lot of ground here, but you will notice a common thread: the first cause of every Power type is invention, be it the invention of a product, process, business model or brand. The adage "'Me too' won't do" guides the creation of Power.

For any business person, "'Me too' won't do" feels right intuitively. Action, creation, risk—these lie at the root of invention. Business value does not start with bloodless analytics. Passion, monomania and domain mastery fuel invention and so are central. The compelling continuing contribution of founders demonstrates this. Planning rarely creates Power. It may meaningfully boost Power once you have established it, but if Power does not yet exist, you can't rely on planning. Instead you must create something new that produces substantial economic gain in the value chain. Not surprisingly, we have worked our way back to Schumpeter.

The Topology of Invention and Power

So what are the elements of this dance of Power and invention? The script usually plays like this:

1. *Flux* in external conditions creates new threats and opportunities. In the case of Netflix, it was both: the eventual decline of their DVD-by-mail business was the threat, and streaming the opportunity.

2. The nature of flux demands that it unfolds in *fits and starts,* so any company wishing to capitalize on these new conditions must invent—again, by crafting, not design. For a single company, these tectonic shifts do not occur frequently, but you can be certain they are coming. The relentless forward march of technology assures this.

3. Amidst this cacophony, you must find a *route to Power.* It wasn't a fine-tuning of their DVD-by-mail business which increased Netflix's market cap by a factor of 100; it was streaming, with its insurmountable Scale Economies.

Building on that, I can now chart the Dynamics of Power:

Figure 8.4: The Dynamics of Power–1

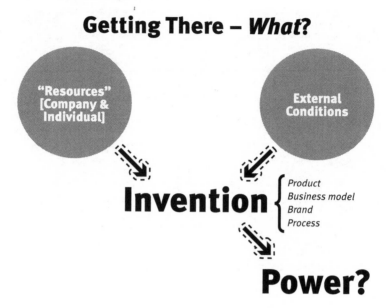

Getting There – *What?*

"Resources"
[Company &
Individual]

External
Conditions

Invention {
Product
Business model
Brand
Process

Power?

Now let's apply this framework to Netflix streaming:[89]

- *Resources.* You must start with the abilities you can bring to bear. Using the academic convention, I will call these "resources." They might be as personal and idiosyncratic as Steve Jobs' aesthetic sensibilities, or as corporate as Google's vast stores of organized data. For Netflix, their original DVD-by-mail business endowed them with numerous resources relevant to streaming, including such directly transferable skills as their recommendation engine, their UI, their customer data and their relationships with content owners. Equally important was the platform of their existing business, which allowed them to easily offer streaming as a complement to DVD-by-mail, rather than a standalone service. This was far more important than you might think, as it silenced potential complaints about the initial small streaming catalogue that could have driven fatally negative word-of-mouth. Conversely, though, there were also many abilities Netflix had to develop, and as they moved aggressively into originals, this set of required competencies expanded considerably.

- *External conditions.* These resources then intersect an opportunity set driven by evolving external conditions: technological, competitive, legal and so on. For Netflix, an advancing technology frontier opened up the potential for streaming: Moore's Law in semiconductors, plus similar exponential advances in optical communications and storage. The embodiments of these trends were high-speed Internet connections, acceptably costed digital storage and a broad dispersion of devices with adequate performance (displays, storage, graphics processing and connectivity). If Netflix had bet the company on streaming any earlier, they would have been dead in the water—external conditions were not yet ripe.

- *Invention.* For Netflix, the inventions were their new product directions: streaming and originals and all the associated complements. Crafted, not designed. Note in Figure 8.4 that the arrows from Resources and External Conditions are dotted not solid. The potential for invention may be there but someone must seize it.

- *Power.* The final step was the thrust into exclusives and originals. By bringing to rein the cost of content, Netflix forged powerful Scale Economies and hence Power. Note also in Figure 8.4 that the connection from Invention to Power is also dotted. Most inventions don't assure Power. As I have discussed, operational excellence—really a constant process of re-invention—does not result in Power.

So if you want to develop Power, your first step is invention: breakthrough products, engaging brands, innovative business models. The first step, yes, but it can't be the last step. Had Netflix invented the streaming product without introducing originals, they would have been left with an easily imitated commodity business. There would have been no Power and little value in the business.

This is where the 7 Powers figures in. In the midst of invention, you need to be ever watchful for Power openings. The 7 Powers framework focuses your attention on the critical issues and increases the odds of a favorable outcome. This is the most Strategy can accomplish. It's not everything, certainly, but it's a lot.

Mintzberg's article threw down the gauntlet: "Can an intellectual discipline meaningfully contribute to a craft?" Or more specifically, "Does Strategy matter to strategy?" Now you know the answer. Yes, it can matter, but only if it works to guide you toward Power in these decisive formative moments. I developed the 7 Powers with exactly this purpose in mind: a practical strategy compass.

Invention: the One-Two Value Punch

So far, so good. By looking through the lens of the 7 Powers, we have come to a vital insight: Power arrives only on the heels of invention. If you want your business to create value, then action and creativity must come foremost.

But success requires more than Power alone; it needs scale. Recall the Fundamental Equation of Strategy:

$$\text{Value} = [\text{Market Size}] * [\text{Power}]$$

In Statics (Part I of this book), rightfully, we focused solely on Power and took market size as a given. Not so with Dynamics. Recall that Netflix's invention (streaming) not only created an opportunity for Power but created the streaming market as well. Both factors must be present to bring about value increases of 100x. Invention has a powerful one-two value punch: it both opens the door for Power and also propels market size.

Figure 8.5: The Dynamics of Power–2

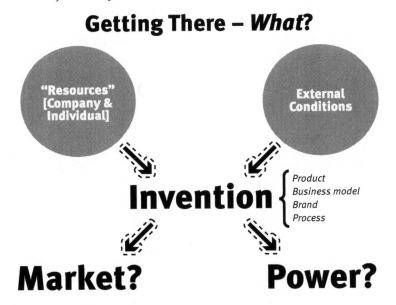

Compelling Value[90]

Invention drives a favorable change in system economics—you get more for less. The resulting gain in the end will be split somehow between your company and other segments of the value chain. The 7 Powers is all about making sure that you get some of the increase. But it is the gain customers experience that will shape the market size. In the Netflix streaming case, if customers hadn't responded favorably to this new delivery mode, then all opportunities for Power would have come to naught. The remainder of this chapter will explore this customer value side. I will use the phrase "compelling value"[91] to characterize products that are sufficiently superior in the eyes of the customer to fuel rapid adoption; they evoke a "gotta have" response. It is this impetus that drives the left-hand side of the FES, market size.

The product differences must be dramatic in order to achieve that "gotta have" response. Just how much is enough? It is tempting to try to attach a number. Andy Grove, the formidable Intel CEO, did just that, suggesting that 10x was in the right ballpark.[92] And it was probably dead-on, at least for the business he was in—semiconductors. But it misses the mark elsewhere. For example, a 50% increase in photovoltaic efficiency, or a battery with double the existing charge-storage density, would both likely clear the bar.

Compelling value requires that you mobilize your capabilities to offer up a product that fulfills a significant customer need currently unmet by competitive offerings. This need drives customer adoption.

Figure 8.6: Compelling Value

Capabilities-Led Compelling Value: Adobe Acrobat

There are three distinct paths to creating compelling value. Each has different tactical needs, so it is instructive to think of them separately. First is *Capabilities-led compelling value*: when a company tries to translate some capability into a product with compelling value.

Figure 8.7: Capabilities-Led Invention

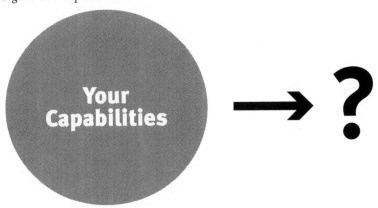

Consider Adobe's creation of Acrobat. Here the key capability brought to bear was Adobe's existing fluency at the intersection of software and graphics. John Warnock, Adobe's co-founder, wanted to utilize this expertise to create a software that enabled the sharing of documents transparently across diverse computer platforms while exactly maintaining visual integrity.

After two intense years of fits and starts, Adobe launched Acrobat 1.0 on June 15, 1993. Acrobat seemed to represent the solution to a vexing problem faced by all corporations: document chaos. As such, anticipation ran rampant:

> ...it was hyped up a lot. Expectations were unbelievably high. It was kinda on the heels of Photoshop, which took off really fast.[93]

But sales in the first year barely cleared $2 million, with the second year not much better. Bob Wulff, the technical lead, kept his job, but the Acrobat general manager slot became a revolving door. Before long, release 2.0 flopped as well.

In the end, the advance of technology (the Internet, in this case) created an unexpected opportunity for Acrobat. HTML, the Internet's enabling language, causes documents to reflow to match the user's platform. Fine in most cases, but there are many documents (presentations and contracts, for example) which depend on preserving the exact look and feel of the original. Acrobat fulfilled this need. By the end of 1996, sales were up to $25 million; by the end of 1998, $58 million. Ten years later, Acrobat had emerged as a nearly billion-dollar business, an important contributor to Adobe's value.

But here's the uncertainty of such a capabilities-led initiative: the customer need is unknown, making such efforts profoundly risky. So risky, in fact, that they should probably be undertaken only if an assured Barrier appears early on. Beware, too: in such cases, the customers' expressions of wants may provide some guidance, but they can prove highly misleading, too. IBM, for instance, had encouraged Adobe early on in its Acrobat endeavor but then balked at the shortcomings of the software. This dynamic is underneath Steve Jobs' remark:

> A lot of times, people don't know what they want until you show it to them.[94]

Success requires that a company stay in the game, appropriately morphing to suit the requirements of the situation. Typically this takes a long time—five years, in Adobe's case—and involves many twists and turns. High testosterone commitments, with all the attendant weight of expectation, should be avoided. If the new business is a standalone one, such commitments will lead to unsustainable external funding requirements, and if the new business has been created by an existing one, such commitments will give rise to the corporate antibodies ever lurking to neutralize new initiatives.

Customer-Led Compelling Value: Corning Fiber Optics

A second path to compelling value is *customer-led compelling value*. In this case, many players spy an unmet need, but no one knows how to satisfy it.

Figure 8.8: Customer-Led Invention

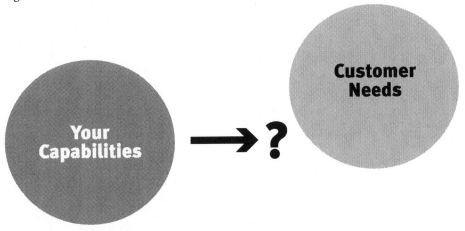

Here Corning's fiber optics provide a good example. By the early 1970s optical fibers—also known as waveguides—had come to be seen as the holy grail of communications, holding the potential to handle vastly increased traffic density. Their creation seemed to carry an assurance of compelling value for any company that could crack the problem. Unfortunately, the transparency demanded of the optical fiber glass was nearly unthinkable: if the ocean matched the clarity required, you could stand over the Marianas Trench and see all the way to the bottom, 35,798 feet below.

More daunting still, Corning was woefully outpaced and under-resourced. Although formidable in glass, the company was new to telecommunications and a pipsqueak next to the other players. Even AT&T, a world leader in telecommunications technology and a behemoth compared to Corning, had lately turned its sights to the prize of optical communications.

Those competitors had opted to follow a quite logical, incremental path in their search for a solution to the transparency problem. They were using the glass formulations already successful in short-distance fiber optics and then trying to tweak them for enhanced clarity. Frank Maurer, an MIT Physics Ph.D. and an old Corning hand, went the other direction. He decided to take pure silica, a glass already known for its clarity, and attempt to make waveguides out of it from scratch. The silica was a very ornery material with a high melting point and high viscosity, but it had two advantages going for it: it was already exceedingly clear from the start, and as a material, it was far more familiar to Corning than anyone else.

Fiber optics are composed of an outer cladding and an inner core, and the physics of the interface between these two keeps the light from "leaking out." Maurer and his two team members, Don Keck and Peter Schultz, faced a big hurdle: how to get silica into the core. After many dead ends, the team finally struck on the idea of using vapor deposition to lay down a uniform film of silica inside the cladding glass.

In September of 1970, Schultz and Keck pulled a full kilometer of fiber. Even though it broke during wrapping, they were left with two great samples. The fiber was ready to test late one Friday afternoon. Schultz had headed home, but Keck was impatient to test the fiber, so worried over its fragility.

> He set up a test jig that aimed a red helium-neon laser beam into the fiber to help him align it. "I remember so vividly moving the fiber over, and when the laser spot hit the core, all of a sudden I got this flash of light"... recalled Keck... [Confused at first,] eventually he realized that the light had gone back and forth through all 200 meters of fiber... He had before him the clearest glass ever made."[95, 96]

Although not the final act of the story, this transparency breakthrough was the development that achieved compelling value. Optical transmission radically reduced the price of a vital human need: interaction at a distance. Fiber optics would quickly become one of the great enabling technologies of the last century, profoundly changing nearly every realm of society: social, industrial, military, academic, etc. The Internet that we know today, of course, would be impossible without fiber optics.

The uncertainty in this case is technical: "Can we invent it?"

Competitor-Led Compelling Value: the Sony PlayStation

The third and final path to compelling value is *competitor-led*. In this case, a competitor has already brought to market a successful product, and the inventor must produce something so much better (in whole product terms) that it elicits the "gotta have" response.

Figure 8.9: Competitor-Led Invention

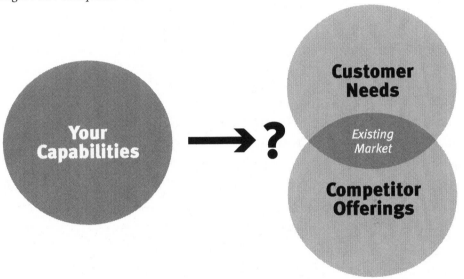

Sony's PlayStation exhibited competitor-led compelling value. In the early 1990s, Sony was an imposing presence in consumer electronics, but a newcomer to video games, facing the formidable established presences of Nintendo and Sega.

Once again, an advancing technology frontier created an opening for a pioneering challenger. An evolutionary product would not have offered much chance of stealing the march on their well-entrenched rivals but Sony's Ken Kutaragi, a brilliant and feisty engineer and the point man for Sony's thrust into video games, was convinced that the breakthrough of real-time 3D graphics would lead to "gotta have." Immersion is the gamer's nirvana, and 3D was a step-change in mimicking reality, eliciting a range of right and left-brain responses that are immune to 2D.

The PlayStation story had many moments of high drama, all of which culminated in the enabling chip order personally guaranteed by Sony President Norio Ohga:

> In May 1993, the Executive Committee heard Tokunaka (Kutaragi's immediate superior) and Kutaragi's presentation and, following Ohga's lead, approved a $50 million investment to develop the computer chip at the heart of the machine, despite the fact that prospects for the new business were at best uncertain… Tokunaka recalls that his hand trembled as he wrote a purchase order for 1.3 million computer chips….[97]

On Dec. 3, 1994, Sony launched the PlayStation in Japan. There were lines around the block. Within a month 300,000 consoles had been sold. At the close of the 1999 fiscal year (March 31), the video game group accounted for 27% of Sony's operating profits. By the time the PlayStation 2 launched in 2000, there was an installed base of 90 million machines, completely eclipsing rival's Nintendo's eighteen million N64 sales and burying poor Sega, which sold only nine million units of its Saturn.[98] Today, as Sony seeks to remake itself, its video game business remains one of its few bright lights.

In cases of competitor-led compelling value, the uncertainty is two-fold: (1) Will the new features be differentially attractive enough to drive share gains? And (2) will the existing competitors be sufficiently delayed in their response?

Competitor-led origination often requires gut-wrenching big bang commitments up front. The time constants are less, and competitive response far more imminent. Often, you must make formal arrangements with providers of complements ahead of time—they will not sign up without such commitments. For example, in the case of the PlayStation, Sony had to make such commitments to independent game companies to ensure they would create games for the platform in the first place. In the case of the iPhone, it was telecommunication giants.

Conclusion

Those two questions—"What must I do?" and "When can I do it?"—hold the key to developing Power in your business. This chapter covered the first question, and shortly in the next chapter, we will tackle the second.

The answer to the "What?" question provides a vital insight into Dynamics: Power comes on the heels of invention, be it in products, processes, brands or business models. However, most invention is merely a manifestation of operational excellence and thus not immune to the arbitraging actions of competition. So in this formative period, as your invention takes shape, you must attune yourself to the exigencies of Power and stay constantly vigilant. This is why I developed the 7 Powers—to give you a ready guide for this.

Steve Jobs famously proselytized for "insanely great products." This was not whimsical, but deeply strategic. Invention not only opens the door to Power, it also fuels market size, the other half of the Fundamental Equation of Strategy.

So let's turn to the complementary question. Now it's time to answer "When?"

Appendix 8.1: Equity Investing and the 7 Powers as a Strategy Compass

In addition to my career as a strategy advisor, I have also been an active equity investor for decades, utilizing the understanding of business value I have gained from Power Dynamics, the full Strategy tool set I have developed which includes the 7 Powers. The Power Dynamics tool set is described in Appendix 10.1. My investment results over this extended period have some relevance to the themes of this book. I have made investments predicated on the differential acuity of the 7 Powers framework in correctly characterizing the prospects for Power in high flux situations. But assessing Power prospects ex ante in high flux situations is also what drives the businessperson's need for a strategy compass. Let me give you some details.

First, to summarize the strategy compass thesis:

- I have made the foundational assumption that Strategy and strategies are about only one thing: potential fundamental business value. I refer to this as the Value Axiom, and it is the bedrock of Power Dynamics and the 7 Powers. This assertion represents an intentional narrowing on my part. The last several decades have proven to me that much acuity and usefulness results from adopting the Value Axiom.

- By far the most important "value moment" for a business occurs when the bars of uncertainty are radically diminished with regards to the Fundamental Equation of Strategy, market size and Power. At that moment, the cash flow future makes a step-change in transparency.

- It is the period of invention, with all its high flux, that gives rise to this "value moment," offering the potential for traction in both market size and Power. High uncertainty persists during this interval because these transitions are typically not linear and quite difficult to forecast accurately.

- Strategy (the discipline) can only contribute in this period if it serves as a strategy compass to guide on-the-ground "inventors," increasing their likelihood of finding a path to satisfy The Mantra.

- To serve as such a cognitive guide, a Strategy framework must be simple but not simplistic. That is the objective of the 7 Powers.

So what relevance does this bear to active equity investing?

To the best of my knowledge, the 7 Powers applies to all businesses, everywhere. Furthermore, it is founded on fundamental business value, which also concerns a large class of investors. Does this mean that utilizing the 7 Powers can result in alpha[99] for investment in any company? Of course not.

In nearly all cases, both the potential for Power and the size of the market are sufficiently evident to astute investment professionals. In particular, they can often be found in the markers of historical financials. Alpha depends on exceptions to the semi-strong form of the Efficient Market Hypothesis: you need material informational advantage. In these cases the 7 Powers offers no such advantage.

The only places one might expect alpha from applying the 7 Powers are those situations in which such transparency is not the case—opacity in other words—and that such opacity is penetrable by the 7 Powers.

A primary driver of opacity is high flux: if a business is in a fast-changing environment, then the information facing investment pros tends to have much higher uncertainty bars regarding future free cash flow. But high flux also attends the sort of conditions which orbit the "value moment." So if the 7 Powers can lead to alpha by identifying Power in these situations *ex ante*, it also promises to be useful in doing the same for those inventors on the ground trying to find a path to satisfy The Mantra.

So how have I done following this approach? Have I been able to deliver alpha? My active investing records go back twenty-two years, but I will be brief in answering those questions. I have daily portfolio returns data for all the 4664 trading days I was in the market, dating from the beginning of 1994 through 2015.[100] My year-by-year annual gross returns are shown in the chart below.

Figure 8.10: Annual Helmer Active Equity Gross Returns (1994–2015)

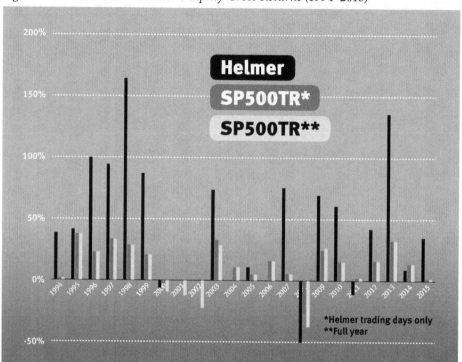

So for these 22 years, I was fully in the market for seventeen years, partially for three years and fully out of the market for two years. For the twenty invested years (seventeen full years and three partial years), my gross returns exceeded those of the market for fourteen years and underperformed the market for six. Over these trading days in which I actively invested, I achieved an average annual rate of return of 41.5%/year versus 14.9%/year for the S&P500 TR. So on average I outperformed the S&P 500TR by 26.6% each year.[101]

However, my highly concentrated approach results in a different risk profile than that of the market overall. So we should also look at a risk-adjusted return.

One way to do so is to take out the effects of the market overall (beta). This yields an average annual alpha of 24.3% (9.1 basis points of alpha per trading alpha day, on average).

Figure 8.11: Risk/Return of Helmer Active Equity Investing

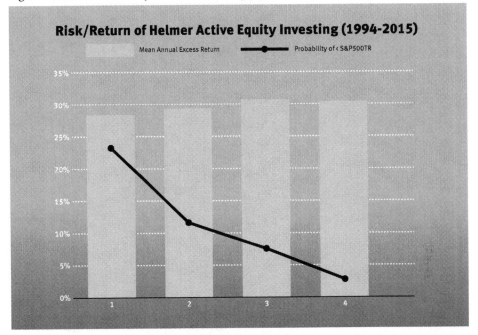

Years Invested

Because of the high concentration,[102] my approach has higher volatility: 31.6% versus 15.8% for SP500TR when annualized. An informative way to assess the risk/reward associated with this is to calculate an investor's prospects of "beating" the market. To do this for all 4664 trading days, I calculated the risk/return profile:

1. *Risk.* What was the probability of underperforming the market if an investor had stayed with my approach for one, two, three and four years?[103]

2. *Return.* What would have been the average annual rate of return over those one, two, three and four year periods?

Figure 8.11 above displays those calculations. This chart would indicate that, historically, if you had invested based on this approach and continued with that investment for 4 years, you would have had about a 3% probability of not outperforming the market (this was your "risk"), and the average return for a four-year hold outperformed the market by about 30%/year (this was your "return").

So based on both these measures, utilizing the 7 Powers has historically delivered unusually attractive returns over an extended period. I know of no other Strategy framework with this outcome. Thus the 7 Powers seems to have been differentially acute as a tool for identifying the potential for Power *ex ante* in high flux situations. This provides additional assurance in its utility as a cognitive frame for business leaders in their crucial "value moments," which are also inevitably high flux.

CHAPTER 9
THE POWER PROGRESSION
TURN, TURN, TURN

Intel Starts from Scratch

In my Introduction I used the case study of Intel to demonstrate the primacy of Power in value creation. Their experience proves particularly revealing because their failed memory business provides a perfect "control" case against which to counterpoint their lucrative microprocessor business.[104] All of Intel's considerable advantages applied in equal measure to both these businesses: unexcelled leadership and management, technical depth, manufacturing prowess, an exploding market, and so on. But the outcomes were utterly different: a painful exit in memories, versus an enduring high-margin business in microprocessors. The difference? One had Power, while the other did not. These two case studies underscore the point: your business must attain Power. Operational excellence by itself is not enough.

In the previous chapter, I addressed the first question of Dynamics: "What does a business have to do to reach that position of Power in the first place?" The understanding reached in that chapter applies full force to Intel—it all started with invention. More specifically, the invention of the microprocessor in fulfillment of a chip design contract with the Japanese calculator company Busicom.[105]

In this chapter I tackle the second question of Dynamics: "*When* can you reach the position of Power?" To start, I will answer this question for Intel's microprocessor business. Building from there, I will go on to derive The Power Progression, a framework for answering the "When?" question for every type of Power. But first, on to Intel.

Intel's route to Power in microprocessors was a slow and tortuous journey. As with most transforming products, the microprocessors business at Intel was marked by dissension and uncertainty. Internally, corporate antibodies were in full force. Bill Graham, the company's gifted head of sales and marketing, threw his full weight toward squelching the microprocessors push—he could not imagine how this business would have the volume to merit draining Intel's scarce cash. The board, too, worried that the diversion would prove too costly, but CEO Bob Noyce and Chairman Arthur Rock carried the day, and Graham lost his battle.

As mentioned above, Intel had originally designed its seminal microprocessor for the Japanese company Busicom, so first they had to buy back the rights to that invention. They succeeded at this, and before long, Intel offered up its earliest commercial microprocessor, the 4004. Then, after some further foot dragging, Intel finally gave its design group full funding, resulting in the 4004's successor, the 8008, in 1972. Further development efforts followed, culminating in 1978 with the breakthrough of the fully 16-bit 8086.

The external challenges were every bit as daunting as the internal ones. On the customer front, the 4004 showed little commercial traction. Semiconductors are a component, not an end product. In such cases, purchase commitments depend on other manufacturers assessing the new component, designing it into their products and then offering those products to consumers. These lags, always significant, were accentuated for microprocessors simply because the product was so radical—not an incremental improvement, but a completely different way of providing computational functionality.

Competitors also proved unexpectedly challenging. The long adoption lead times for the technology gave rivals ample time to build on Intel's experience and develop products of their own. In late 1978, Intel was rocked on its heels to find that, rather than leading the pack, they were losing design wins. Even Intel insiders conceded that the Motorola 68000 was a superior product. The competitive dynamic that was wrecking their memory business now threatened microprocessors as well.

Intel responded with the aggressiveness forged into the company by Andy Grove, launching Operation Crush, an audacious frontal assault in sales and marketing. Intel leadership set a wildly aggressive target of 2000 design wins within the year, and the company set to work executing this corporate-wide crusade.

The intense push motivated Inteler Earl Whetstone to try a long-shot sales prospect: IBM. Up until then, most had assumed that IBM would internally source any significant semiconductor needs. The company had its own microprocessor, the IBM 801 RISC, which was far more powerful than the 8086, plus its own internal semiconductor manufacturing system, which was larger than any of the stand-alone semiconductor firms.

But times had changed for IBM. They had missed the minicomputer boom; their overall share of the computer market had shrunk considerably, and their stock was off. This chastening opened minds to new methods of doing business, eventually resulting in Project Chess, a well-funded effort to develop a personal computer within only a year.

To keep costs low and minimize delays, IBM abandoned all sorts of usual practices, and so it was that Intel's Whetstone found, to his immense surprise, a welcoming attitude in Don Estridge, the newly tapped leader of Project Chess in Boca Raton, Florida.

With a herculean effort Estridge and his team met their one-year deadline, developing the revolutionary IBM PC, which included the Intel 8088, a dumbed-down version of the 8086. No one could have anticipated the market explosion that followed. The IBM PC rolled out on August 12, 1981. Over the next year, it sold 750,000 units.[106] Every one of these came with an Intel 8088. Here, at last, came the mother lode application for Intel's microprocessors.

From Invention to Power

Below is a chart of Intel's stock price from the time of the 8088 design win until the end of 2015.

Figure 9.1: Intel Stock Price vs. S&P 500 (Index Value: 3/17/1980 = 1.00)[107]

Over this period, Intel's market cap soared to the rarefied air of over $100B and stayed there. Its stock price increased more than 8500%, compared to the approximate 2000% increase of the S&P 500. All of this value came from their microprocessor business. More specifically, it resulted from three of the 7 Powers:[108]

1. *Scale Economies.* Piggy-backing on the rocket ship of the IBM PC, Intel achieved a large advantage in scale that it has never given up. This enables lower per-unit costs in several ways:

   • **Fixed cost of chip design.** The costs of semiconductor design are high. Intel is able to prorate this fixed cost over a far higher volume, dramatically lowering the per-unit design cost.

- **Fixed factory design costs.** Semiconductor plants (fabs) are complex and expensive. Intel's approach utilizes a single design, so fab design cost is prorated across many fabs, again resulting in lower costs per chip.

- **Early movers in lithography advances.** Each generation of semiconductors moves to smaller-scale features. This enables significant manufacturing and product efficiencies. By virtue of its higher demand forecasts, Intel is able to justify moving a fab to the smaller etch widths sooner, further enhancing their per-chip cost advantage at any given moment.

2. *Network Economies.* Consumers don't buy *just* chips; they don't even buy *just* PCs. When buying a personal computer, what they're really purchasing is this: the ability to do certain tasks which are enabled by applications running on PCs, meaning software and hardware go hand in glove; they are complements. In the early years of consumer PC sales, because of the memory and speed limitations of chips, operating systems and some applications had to be programmed specifically for the processor. In particular, the program that launched the IBM PC, the spreadsheet Lotus 123, was written specially for the Intel processor, as was the operating system MS-DOS that was provided by Microsoft. This meant that when other PC makers came on line, they had to utilize IBM clones, or else they would have no programs. This meant that they used Intel, or Intel-compatible, chips. Network Economies were in force.

3. *Switching Costs.* If you owned a PC and were considering a switch to something else, the same chip-specific programming would stop you from moving to a non-Intel machine. Otherwise, all the hours of toil you had put into your current programs would be unusable.

In time, OS and application software became abstracted from the chip level, largely eviscerating any Network Economies, but by that point Intel had achieved a huge scale advantage. My former partner Bill Mitchell put it well:

> "The one-sentence story of Intel is a single design win, then a decade and a half of very high Switching Costs, then Scale Economies."[109]

How exactly did Intel get there for each of their sources of Power?

- *Scale Economies.* To establish this advantage, Intel seized the required market share lead by the end of the explosive growth stage of the PC market. Once growth settles down, the stakes are well known, and the volume leader can and will use their cost advantage to fend off competitors.

- *Network Economies.* The importance of the takeoff stage is even more pronounced with Network Economies. Network Economies are often characterized by a tipping point: once the leader has achieved an edge in installed base, most users will find it to their benefit to choose that leader. For application software developers, the choice of attractive microcomputer platforms was winnowed to only two choices with sufficient scale: Apple and PCs. Lacking in competitive applications, other platforms were doomed.

- *Switching Costs.* Even for Switching Costs, takeoff is the critical stage: first off, Switching Costs are a source of Power for those who get to the customer first, and a wealth of customer relationships are established in the takeoff; secondly, in the takeoff period, customers are often struggling to find any supplier, so the price competition that will eventually arbitrage out the value of switching costs for new customers has yet to occur.

The Power Progression: Takeoff

So there we have it: all of Intel's sources of Power were rooted in the takeoff period. Again, takeoff is the stage when differential customer acquisition can take place at favorable terms, which is why it presents such ideal Power opportunities. There is such a high degree of flux that the normal lags in the arbitraging process are material to the outcome: resolving uncertainty, transparency, product tuning, building capacity, establishing channels, effective marketing and so on. For Intel, Operation Crush made a crucial difference to Power. In a mature business, it would have simply been part of the to-and-fro of arbitrage.

What cut-off point in the growth rate marks the end of this takeoff period? It depends on the degree of flux and uncertainty, but based on my experience,

30–40%/year seems a workable choice. By this measure, for the PC market, takeoff probably started in 1975 with the 8080 and continued through 1983.

Figure 9.2: Annual Growth of Microcomputer Shipments (units)[110]

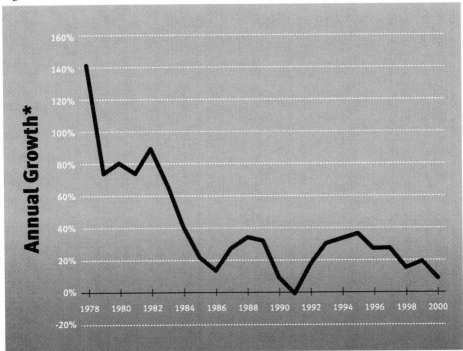

*three-year moving average

Armed with this understanding, you can see that Intel made it in just under the wire. They made a decisive break from the peloton of competitors at a crucial time. If the PC market had forged ahead for another year or two without them, the window of opportunity would surely have closed—no breakaway would have been possible. Intel would have captured some sales, but their prospects for Power would have dimmed as the opportunity for Scale Economies quickly receded. Put into context, if another company had won the IBM contract, Intel as we know it today would not exist.

This sort of situation breeds a common form of false positive. Often in the explosive growth stage, companies will exhibit quite attractive financials. The future looks bright. Long-term success seems assured. Unfortunately, if a company has not established Power, competitive arbitrage will catch up as soon as growth slows; fundamentals will assert themselves, and the favorable early returns will prove fleeting. As a strategist and value investor, I cringe every time a CEO or CFO says they are pleased by the entrance into their market of a well-heeled competitor, insisting it "validates the market." In 1981, at the introduction of the IBM PC, Apple had the temerity to run a large ad in the *Wall Street Journal*: "**Welcome, IBM. Seriously.**" They did not understand the nature of Power attainment in the takeoff stage: you and your competitor are in a race for relative scale, and there can only be one winner.

Intel's experience imparts a crucial "When?" lesson: the takeoff period represents a singular time. Only then can you initiate three important types of Power: Scale Economies, Network Economies and Switching Costs. If unrealized, these opportunities disappear forever afterward.

The Clock for the Power Progression

Given the critical importance of takeoff for establishing Power, the clock for calibrating the acquisition of Power should be parsed into three time windows—before, during and after takeoff:

> *Stage 1: Before—Origination.* This occurs before a company clears the compelling value threshold, at which time sales rapidly pick up pace. For microprocessors, the entire Busicom period, including Intel's efforts up until the release of the 8080, constituted the Origination stage.

> *Stage 2: During—Takeoff.* This is the period of explosive growth.

> *Stage 3: After—Stability.* The business may still be growing considerably, but growth has slowed from "explosive" levels, with 30–40% per-year unit growth as a workable choice for the cutoff. Above this rate, the market doubles in two years, sufficiently

fluid for market leadership swaps without value-destroying counter-moves.

A word of caution: parsing by growth should not create the impression that the phases above are congruent with the well-known product life cycle stages of introduction, growth, maturity and decline. They do not align, and the differences are critical. First of all, the three stages described above are defined by the metric of company growth, not market growth. Company growth best reflects the degree of flux faced by *that company*. Secondly, the breakpoints are entirely different: the origination stage precedes these familiar product life cycle stages and may exhibit no sales for a long time; stability, on the other hand, features considerable growth, and so it overlaps all of the last three stages of the life cycle model. My parsing utilizes takeoff to delineate stages. When trying to discern the availability of Power, this grouping proves essential. The product life cycle grouping will not serve this purpose.

Bearing this in mind, I can now tackle the challenge laid down at the beginning of this chapter: "Can one meaningfully generalize about *when* Power is established?" I will use the same methodology as Chapter 8, parsing the question by Power type: "For each of the 7 Powers, must they be established in origination, takeoff or stability?"

Distilling it further, what I am really asking is this: "When must one establish the Barrier?" Power results from the simultaneous presence of a Benefit and a Barrier. Both of these play a pivotal role in Dynamics. Chapter 8 demonstrated the vital role of invention in implanting Benefits and forging the potential for Power. But as I have discussed throughout this book, Benefits are common, and they often bear little positive impact on company value, as they are generally subject to full arbitrage. The true potential for value lies in those rare instances in which you can *prevent* such arbitrage, and it is the Barrier which accomplishes this. Thus, the decisive attainment of Power often syncs up with the establishment of the Barrier.

The Power Progression maps this Barrier timing. For the Intel example previously discussed:

Figure 9.3

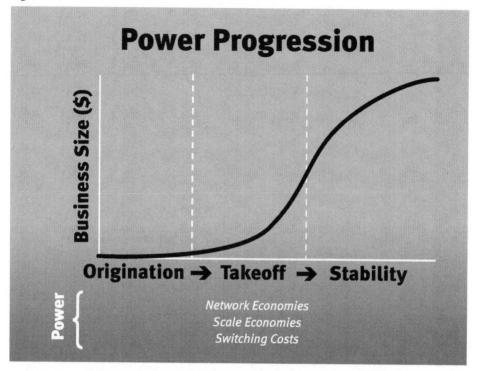

The Power Progression maps when Power must be **established** by Power type. It indicates at what point the window is open. Intel's three Power types continued on into the stability phase, of course; that's why the company's value has endured. However, if Intel had not established Scale Economies, Network Economies or Switching Costs by the time they reached stability, the possibility of Power would have vanished forever. They would have likely become a low-margin electronic components company, a relentless treadmill fate that awaited many other semiconductor firms, including the Japanese juggernauts that trumped Intel in the memory business only years before.

The Power Progression: Origination

Now let's turn our attention to the origination stage that occurs before takeoff. There are two types of Power that typically become first available during this earlier period.

Cornered Resource. The crucial step in Intel's microprocessor victory came when they reacquired the rights to their invention from Busicom, which they accomplished three years prior to takeoff. Had Intel not regained these microprocessor rights, another company would have wielded this Power over them, possibly preventing them from ever entering this business.

A good case can also be made for another pre-takeoff Cornered Resource at Intel: the potent triumvirate of Bob Noyce, Gordon Moore and Andy Grove. Arthur Rock once said that Intel needed Noyce, Moore and Grove in that order, and Rock eagerly put his money where his mouth was. Perhaps, in their absence, other leaders or managers might have stepped up to the plate, but it is hard to imagine Intel's success without all three. All were deeply technically able, but each brought to the table a talent the others lacked. Noyce's visionary leadership proved essential in spotting the potential of microprocessors and then backing them. Moore's deep scientific chops helped solve the early and serious production problems of semiconductors. Grove's implacable focus on execution drove Intel to a level of excellence that might have otherwise eluded them. Putting three such competencies together in a functioning senior management team would be a hard challenge, especially for a start-up.

Indeed, pre-takeoff Cornered Resources underlie many important transforming successes. For example, drug patents form the foundation of the branded pharmaceutical business, whose transforming successes have created hundreds of billions in shareholder value. The promise of this type of Power, secure from the start, is what underlies the industry's willingness to pour billions into high-risk research efforts.[111]

Counter-Positioning. Counter-Positioning requires the invention of an attractive business model that presents a vexing "damned if you do/damned if you don't" cul-de-sac for incumbents. It is this business model's whole product that creates the takeoff for the challenger, so it must precede that phase and occur during origination.

Thus Counter-Positioning and Cornered Resource are most likely to be established in the origination stage. These are wonderful, durable types of Power specifically because your "route to Power" is locked in early, so long as you execute well. I have mapped these two onto the Power Progression below.

Figure 9.4

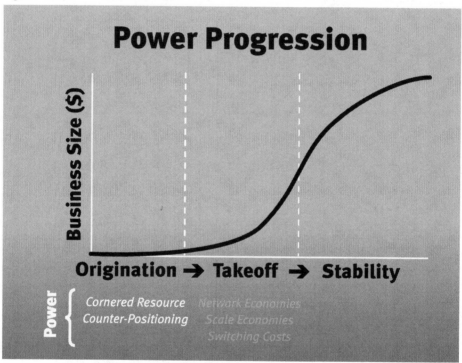

The Power Progression: Stability

Finally, there are two types of Power that are likely to be established in the stability stage.

> **Process Power.** Process Power occurs if a company over time develops a significantly superior internal process which competitors cannot emulate easily. Process Power typically avails itself only in the stability stage. Why then? Because only when a company has scaled sufficiently and operated long enough can it have evolved processes which are sufficiently complex or opaque to defy speedy emulation.[112]

> **Branding.** With Branding in the mix, there is only one Barrier of consequence: the long time and uncertainty a challenger would face in emulation. Think of the steep slope a new entrant would face against Hermès, with their many decades of carefully cultivated quality and exclusivity. Because this long path serves as a defining characteristic, the opportunity for Branding must be squarely placed in the stability stage. Prior to that, there just hasn't been enough time to thoughtfully cultivate the necessary associations.

You might lull yourself into thinking that there are opportunities for Branding in the origination phase. Perhaps your existing brand is considering some transforming initiative, a thrust into an entirely new arena of business? You reasonably assume the brand's reputation can provide significant pricing Power from the start. Use caution: this is possible, but rare. Consider such failures as Hermès Cognac or Porsche sunglasses. Perhaps the most notable exception would be Disney's move into theme parks. But again, such cases are rare.

Figure 9.5

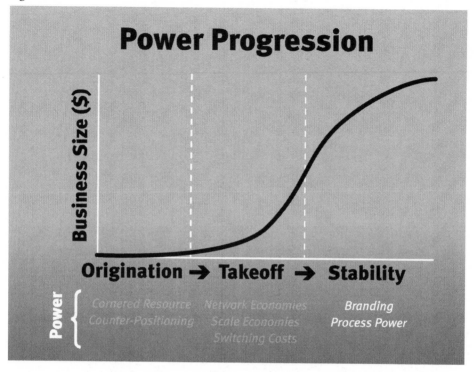

This then fully populates the Power Progression, which answers the question "For each of the 7 Powers, when does Power first become available?" This is a potent shorthand, because it enables you to quickly narrow your search for Power to only those types that map to the growth stage your business is currently in.

The Power Progression provides another solid instantiation of Professor Porter's insight to understand Statics before tackling Dynamics. This crucial question of the timing of strategy windows can only be meaningfully answered by asking it for individual Power types, and these types are revealed by Statics.

The Time Character of the Four Barriers

Let's now delineate by time the 7 Powers Chart developed earlier.

Figure 9.6: Time-Delineated 7 Powers

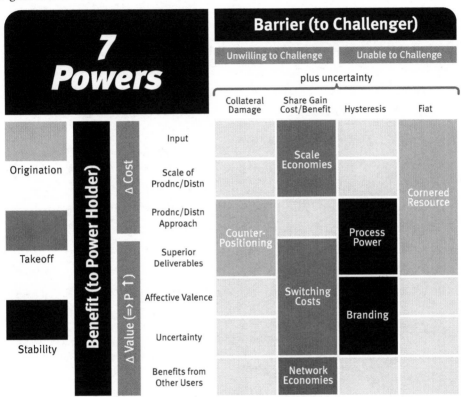

This pulls into focus another Dynamics insight: each of the four generic Barriers is specific to stage. This results from the nature of those barriers:

- *Hysteresis.* The Barrier here? A structural time constant facing all players. It makes sense, then, that all Powers relying on hysteresis would only become available in the stability stage, as the takeoff stage is relatively short-lived and does not usually provide sufficient time to build up the Benefit, constrained as it is by the time constant.

- *Collateral Damage.* Here it is the economics of the challenger's business model which threatens collateral damage to the incumbent. But, the initiation of this business model is what gets the challenger off the ground so it must occur in origination.

- *Fiat.* The critical issue here concerns whether the "right" protected by fiat is fully priced. As the business proposition involving the Cornered Resource develops during takeoff, the resource's value becomes more widely known, substantially reducing the probability that it will be materially underpriced, and it must be underpriced to qualify as a Cornered Resource.

- *Cost of Gaining Share.* Of course the whole notion of gaining share carries no meaning in the origination stage, as sales have not yet materialized. When the business takes off, there are many factors which determine which company can scale most rapidly: channel position, product features, communication approaches, location, production constraints, etc. As a consequence, the "price" of share usually does not reflect its intrinsic long-term value. Upon reaching the stability stage, the most effective modalities become better known and accessible to many players. There the customer's focus turns from "Can I get it?" to "What is the best deal?" In this situation, each player grasps the value of share and will game accordingly, usually arbitraging out its value. Hence, generally speaking, only in the takeoff stage can a player gain share on attractive terms; otherwise it is too costly to be worthwhile.

The Power Progression—the Data (Frequency Histogram of Power Type)

So far I have relied upon theory, supported by anecdote, to develop the Power Progression. To provide some empirical validation, I turned to the research of my students, as for the last seven years I have been teaching business strategy in the Economics Department at Stanford University. I had a team review the instances of Power in all the research papers of my students to determine at what stage at which Power first occurred. The frequency histogram below displays the results of this distillation.

Figure 9.7

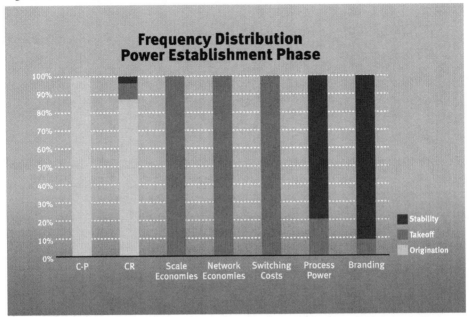

This histogram lends strong support to the stage timing of Power developed earlier. There are exceptions, but by and large the Power Progression is borne out:

- Origination: Counter-Positioning and Cornered Resource

- Takeoff: Scale Economies, Network Economies and Switching Costs

- Stability: Process Power and Branding

The Dynamics Difference

In moving from Statics to Dynamics, scope is broadened considerably. At a high level, we see that in the fundamental equation of Strategy:

$$\textbf{Value} = \textbf{M}_0 \; \textbf{\textit{g}} \; \bar{\textbf{\textit{s}}} \; \overline{\textbf{\textit{m}}}$$

Statics concerned itself only with Power and hence just the last two terms ($\bar{s}$, market share, and, $\overline{m}$, differential margins); primarily, it focused on just one ($\overline{m}$).

In contrast, in a Dynamics context, a company can profoundly influence both the two market size terms (M_0, the current market size, and g, the discounted growth factor). The creation of compelling value, for example, is joined at the hip to the creation of a market. In the lingo of economists: in Statics M_0 and g are taken as exogenous, whereas in Dynamics they are endogenous.

This broadening of scope also applies to many particulars as well. Here's one of great import: operational excellence. In my Statics discussion, I explained why operational excellence is not strategic—because it's imitable, and therefore subject to competitive arbitrage. In the high flux shortened time frame of the takeoff Stage, sufficiently timely imitation becomes less likely, and excellent execution can be highly strategic.

Consider, for example, Apple's trajectory. The Apple II was released in 1977, and paired with VisiCalc software, it rocketed ahead, seemingly poised to own its space. The follow-on Apple III was released on May 19, 1980, fifteen months before the IBM PC. Unfortunately the product was a dog, and it couldn't even roll over, although it did a pretty good "play dead." The Apple III had been manufactured utilizing an immature circuit board technology, so short circuits plagued the product from the start. At one point, Apple even released a technical bulletin instructing customers to drop their computers from a height of three inches to try to reseat dislodged chips. To make matters worse, it was a pricey box, starting at over $4000 and going up to almost $8000 fully loaded. Only a year later, the IBM PC was offered at $1600.

The Apple III bombed—right at the very moment when a killer product would have propelled Apple to a near-insurmountable preeminence. Not only that. Since Apple controlled the OS, their microcomputer business could have become a high Power one. Instead, that business never recovered. Apple had flubbed the takeoff period. For a while, they maintained a respectable business and continued to be the innovation leader, but these setbacks put them on the road to an ever-declining share in personal computers, and an eventual near-death experience that could only have been reversed by the genius of a resurgent Steve Jobs.

Operational excellence was crucial, and its lack caused Apple to fumble. For Intel, and their microprocessor business, it was very much the converse. Without

Operation Crush, it seems likely to me that Intel would have missed the IBM PC opportunity and with it the chance to achieve an utterly dominant relative scale advantage.

Operation Crush reveals another telling difference between a Statics view and a Dynamics view—the role of leadership. As a value investor, I consider Warren Buffett one of my heroes. I previously mentioned his insight that good managers can rarely reverse the course of a bad business, i.e. one without Power. Over and over, I have witnessed Buffett's axiom play out in the press, with business leaders castigated for poor management ability in the face of seemingly impossible circumstances. Yahoo, Twitter and Zynga come to mind here. That said, when it comes to establishing Power in the first place, make no mistake: leadership is fundamental. Operation Crush would never have happened were it not for Andy Grove's implacable, aggressive leadership. Going back further, the company would not have even pursued microprocessors were it not for the leadership of Bob Noyce.

In summary, when you step back to consider how Power is established in the first place, there are a lot more parts to the puzzle: leadership, timing, execution, cleverness and luck can all play decisive roles.

Conclusion: The Strategy Compass and 7 Powers

As I have underscored throughout these pages, Strategy's highest calling must be to serve as a real-time strategy compass. To fulfill this role, it must be distilled into a framework that is simple but not simplistic.

The first seven chapters built, brick by brick, the 7 Powers. This is your strategy compass. Then in the final two chapters I addressed the "What?" and "When?" to clarify the terrain you are navigating with your compass.

With these ideas as your toolkit, you are now fully prepared to blaze your own path to satisfying The Mantra:

A route to continuing Power in significant markets.

This is what strategy means and this is what you must achieve to be a success.

Appendix 10.1: The Power Dynamics Toolkit

The body of Strategy intellectual capital I have developed is called Power Dynamics. The 7 Powers is its central unifying framework. Overall Power Dynamics is built on and tied tightly to seven perspectives.

1. **The Value Axiom.** Strategy has one and only one objective: maximizing potential fundamental business value.

Commentary. This is an assumption not a proof. My experience is that this narrowing of the scope of Strategy and strategy has a profoundly positive impact on the usefulness of the discipline. Note that this is fundamental not speculative value. Further it is about potential value. Realizing that value requires operational excellence.

2. **The 3 S's.** Power, the potential to realize persistent differential returns, is the key to value creation. Power is created if a business attribute is simultaneously:

   • Superior—improves free cash flow

   • Significant—the cash flow improvement must be material

   • Sustainable—the improvement must be largely immune to competitive arbitrage

Commentary. In this book I have focused on Benefit + Barrier which has a one-to-one mapping to the 3 S's (Superior + Significant = Benefit and Sustainable = Barrier). However, in the field, the tripartite 3 S test of Power proves useful additionally because, since it calls out "Significant" separately, it makes materiality explicit. For example, businesses often tout network effects but, when looked at carefully, they are not material and therefore do not qualify as Power.

3. **The Fundamental Equation of Strategy. Value = $M_0 \, g \, \bar{s} \, \bar{m}$**

Commentary. The interpretation of this is that Value = Market Size * Power. M_0 is the current market size, g is a discounted growth factor for the market, $\bar{s}$ is long-term average market share and $\bar{m}$ is long-term average differential margins (the profit margin above that needed to return the cost of capital). I have found that the explicit tying of Strategy concepts to the exact determinants of the net present value of free cash flow puts to rest a lot of fuzzy thinking about the relationship between Strategy and value. It has also helped me as an active equity investor. It is important that $\bar{s}$ and $\overline{m}$ are long-term equilibrium values. Short-term movements in these have little impact on fundamental value.

4. **The Mantra.** A route to continuing Power in significant markets.

Commentary. If you only take one phrase away from reading this book, I hope it is this one. It is a complete statement of the elements of a strategy. It maps directly to the Fundamental Equation of Strategy and is inclusive of Dynamics. The word "continuing" is included, even though Power implies sustainability, to encourage ongoing layering on of different sources of Power as a business progresses.

5. **The 7 Powers.**

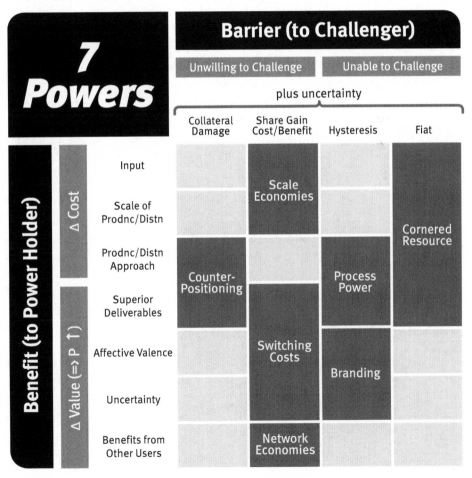

Commentary. To the best of my knowledge the seven Power types positioned on this chart are the only strategies available to a company. If you do not have at least one of these for each competitor (current and potential, direct and functional), you cannot satisfy The Mantra and hence are lacking a viable strategy. In the 200+ strategy cases I have led over my career, these seven were sufficient. This is also true of all the cases studied by my students, probably another 200 or so.

Aside from being exhaustive, two additional characteristics of the 7 Powers enhance its usefulness:

a. *Small set.* The key strategic questions for you are: (1) "What Power types do I now have?" and (2) "What Power types do I need to worry about establishing now?" The 7 Powers informs you that there are only seven possibilities for (1) and usually you can quickly rule out several. The Power Progression informs you that at any given growth stage the maximum number of new Powers that you might explore is 3. This focusing is very valuable. If you cannot see a route to one of these 7, your strategy problem is not yet solved.

b. *Observable ex ante.* The potential for these Power types is usually evident long before detailed forecasting is possible. What I have found working with early-stage companies in Silicon Valley and working with mature companies considering new directions is that it is possible to have meaningful conversations about the potential for Power at quite an early stage.[113] My investment results are also indicative of this *ex ante* transparency.

6. **"Me Too" Won't Do.** The first cause of a strategy is invention.

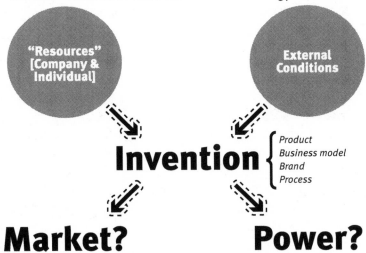

Invention {
Product
Business model
Brand
Process
}

Commentary. Tectonic changes in value take place when Power is first established with an acceptable level of certainty. Looking at the seven Power types we can see that this always involves an invention, whether that be an invention of product, business model, process or brand. Eventually such inventions lead to a Benefit as expressed in a product attribute, be that features, price or reliability. The marker for sufficiency of such a Benefit is usually "compelling value," eliciting a "gotta have" response. There are three paths to achieving compelling value: Capabilities-led, Customer-led and Competitor-led. These each present distinctly different tactical imperatives.

My view is that there is an important welfare implication in these relationships as well. Not only is invention the gateway to Power but also the possibility of Power (and the associated durable success) fuels invention. For example, if there were no prospects for Power then I doubt that Silicon Valley would have come to be. So from a static viewpoint, the search for Power may seem like a zero sum game of preventing gains flowing to consumers. But from a Dynamics viewpoint, it is the possibility of Power that is a critical motivator of invention. An invention only gains traction if customers flock to it. This take-up is of course a sure marker of increases in consumer welfare—they are voting with their feet. This Dynamics perspective is of course the one that should motivate policy makers.

7. **The Power Progression.**

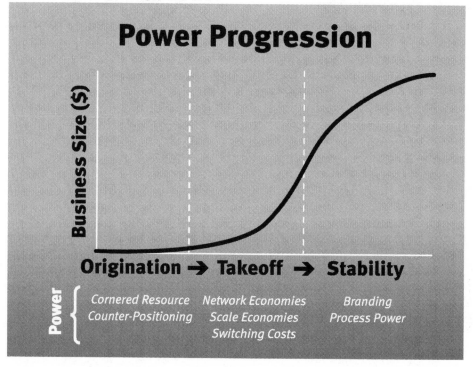

Commentary. Different Power types present the opportunity for first establishing a Barrier at different times in the development of your business. Knowing when this window is open and when it shuts is valuable in recognizing and seizing the opportunity. The break between takeoff and stability is when unit growth falls below about 30%–40%/year. This is a business stage framework and should not be confused with the product stages of Introduction/Growth/Maturity/Decline of the Product Life Cycle which have dramatically different points of phase separation. Origination can include pre-product periods which are not covered in the Life Cycle model, and the Growth stage in the Life Cycle model includes takeoff and parts of stability in the Power Progression. These differences really matter in assessing the availability of Power.

Appendix 10.2: A graphical representation of the tools of Power Dynamics and their relationship.

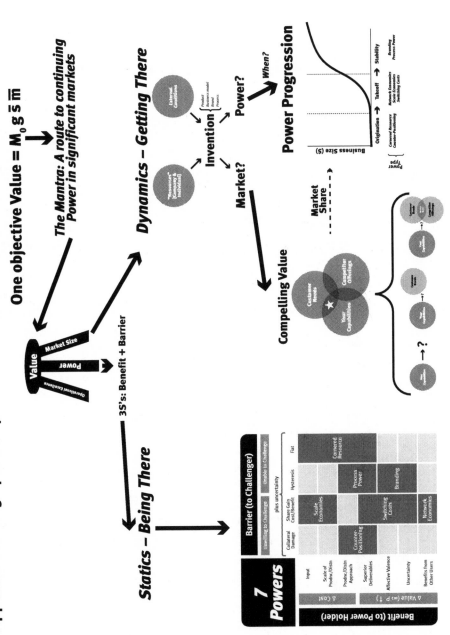

Appendix 10.3: Power Dynamics Glossary

Term	Description
Strategy	Strategy (with a Capital S) is the intellectual discipline sometimes called Strategic Management. I define it: the study of the fundamental determinants of potential business value.
Power	The set of conditions needed for persistent differential returns. Power requires both a Benefit, something that materially increases cash flow, and a Barrier, conditions such that all the value to the firm of the Benefit is not arbitraged out by competition.
strategy	Strategy (with a lower case s) is the path to potential value for a strategically separate business. I define it: a route to continuing Power in significant markets.
value	The fundamental enterprise value of an activity. This is reflected *ex post* as generation of accessible returns to an owner (free cash flow). It is investors' expectation of the stream of these returns discounted over time that determines value *ex ante*.
Strategy Dynamics	The study of strategy development over time.
Strategy Statics	The study of strategic position at a single point in time.
industry	The group of businesses whose products have a high degree of substitutability.
business	A strategically separate economic activity within a single firm. By strategically separate I mean that its Power position is largely orthogonal to the Power position of other activities the firm pursues.
market	The revenue attributable to all firms in a business (the industry).

Term	Description
industry economics	The economic structure of a particular industry. For example, with fixed-cost-driven Scale Economies, this is measured by the magnitude of the fixed cost relative to the company's overall financials.
competitive position	A characterization of a company position in the metric relevant to Power. For example, with Scale Economies it is relative scale compared to the largest competitor.
Surplus Leader Margin	The profit margin a Power holder will achieve if pricing is such that a firm in the same business with no Power has zero profits. This is not necessarily an expected equilibrium but rather is a good marker of the leverage possessed by the Power holder. This would equal $\overline{m}$ in the Fundamental Equation of Strategy if the firm without Power experienced competitive arbitrage that resulted in its earning just its cost of capital and that the cost of capital for the firm with Power was equal to the cost of capital of the firm without Power.

ACKNOWLEDGMENTS

This book distills what I have learned about Strategy over decades of consulting, investing and teaching. Throughout the years, I have interacted with, and benefited from, so many thoughtful people that I am at a loss to name them all. I will mention some, but for those left out, I ask forbearance.

First I must thank my Stanford co-conspirator on this project, Pai-Ling Yin. Pai-Ling is a deeply thoughtful Strategy scholar, and our many fascinating conversations greatly advanced my thinking. At one time, she signed on to serve as co-author of this book, and even developed early drafts of three chapters. Unfortunately, her work demands required that she back out of the project. Even still, her many insights have left a lasting impact on the effort.

My editor Blair Kroeber has been with me every step of the way—there is not a paragraph in this book which he hasn't carefully reviewed. Always a pleasure to work with, he has proven quite extraordinary in his ability to polish my prose while preserving my voice and remaining true to my logic. This would have been a different book without his help.

I owe an intellectual debt to the numerous consulting clients I have served over the years. The problems they posed have been foundational to my understanding of Strategy. During these decades of work, there are some individuals who stand out in my memory as being exceptionally stimulating and congenial: Denis Brown of Pinkerton, Derek Chilvers of John Hancock, Bruce Chizen and

Bryan Lamkin of Adobe, Bill Hanley of Galileo Elector-Optics, Reed Hastings of Netflix, Greg Hinckley of Mentor Graphics, John Meyers of Hewlett-Packard, Jim Putnam of Markem, Mark Thompson of Raychem, and Bob Wilson of Southwall Technologies. Each has been such a pleasure to work with. Their on-the-ground experience and their probing intelligence focused my thinking in ways otherwise impossible.

The acuity, hard work and enthusiasm of my many accomplished Stanford students have provided constant inspiration to me. The challenge of conveying to them the complex discipline of Strategy has considerably sharpened my concepts. Further, many participated in research teams I organized on topics germane to this book. Their efforts have made a real contribution to the understandings presented in *7 Powers*. It has been my great pleasure to be their teacher.

The Economics Department at Stanford has been unusually supportive as well. Unlike my talented colleagues there, I did not follow the path of an academic Economist; nevertheless, my course has been openly welcomed within the Department, and I have been given the freedom to teach it the way I see fit. I want to especially thank my Yale classmate John Shoven, who first introduced to Stanford the idea of my teaching there. John recently retired as the Director of SIEPR, but the legacy of his leadership there is profound. I also wish to thank Larry Goulder, who was Department Chair when I first began teaching at Stanford. Larry got me off to a great start with his thoughtful support and general openness to my approach.

I was fortunate enough to work for Bain & Company right out of graduate school, and that's where my lifelong passion for Strategy ignited. Nowadays such a career track isn't all that unusual for an Economics Ph.D.; back then, however, it was completely untrod. Bill Bain placed a bet on me, and for that I am forever in his debt. During my initial job interview, I discussed with him a concern I had heard from other interviewers—namely, that I lacked an MBA. His counsel: "Don't worry, I don't have one either." Bain & Company quickly proved a perfect place for me to work. Surrounded by sharp peers, guided by more experienced hands, I was able to immerse myself in one fascinating problem after another. My current Strategy Capital partner, John Rutherford, served as an especially thoughtful guide in those early days.

Yale has a world-class Economics Department, but it's also an inordinately humane and welcoming institution. While there, I was privileged to count Bill Parker as my friend, mentor and eventual thesis committee chair. Bill was a deep humanist, blessed with a penetrating wry wit—heaven help the pompous around Bill Parker! I am also grateful to know Bill Brainard, whose Microeconomic Theory course I took during my first term at Yale. His brilliance and compelling teaching were inspirational to me then, and remain so to this day, even though I now possess only the barest recall of bordered Hessians.

The book was improved by a number of readers who were kind enough to look over portions of it and offer their suggestions: Blake Grossman (the prior CEO of Barclays Global Investors) and Mike Latham (the prior COO of iShares) for my chapter on Counter-Positioning; Jeff Epstein (the prior CFO of Oracle) for my chapter on Switching Costs; Larry Tint (the Chairman of Quantal International) for my Appendix to Chapter 8; Pete Docter (Pixar feature-film director) for my chapter on Cornered Resources; Wally Rhines (CEO of Mentor Graphics) and Bill Mitchell (Portfolio Manager of Spinoff & Reorg Fund) on Intel; Reed Hastings (CEO of Netflix) for the Introduction; Daphne Koller (Co-Founder and past President of Coursera) for overall book comments. While I cannot hold them responsible for any errors I might have made, their insights improved the content of these pages.

I have had an exemplary production team for this book: 1106 Design for the overall layout, Rebecca Bloom for copy-editing, Irene Young for cover design and web layout and Katherine Evers (one of my Stanford students) for developing displays. They have conducted themselves with grace and professionalism throughout the book's long gestation period.

This book opens with a dedication to my family and so it should end with an acknowledgement of them. First, my wife Lalia, who constantly encouraged me during the lean years in which I established my consulting firm, and who has fully supported my single-minded commitment to advancing Strategy concepts. We have never taken a vacation in which she didn't make a point of confirming that the potential venue included a quiet place for me think—in fact, I concocted the 7 Powers construct while on a tranquil beach in Mexico! My three children have also contributed materially. My daughter Margaret cast her eagle eye to the overall visuals of the book, and brought her aesthetic insights to bear on it throughout.

My son Edmund offered advice on graphics and suggested the subtitle of the book. My son Andrew carefully read over the whole book, flagging numerous typos, but also helping to refine the reasoning in several spots. I have been blessed with their love and support.

BIBLIOGRAPHY

There has been a great deal of fine work in the academic world on Strategy, or Strategic Management, as it is called in those circles. If the reader wishes to explore that work, these excellent bibliographies offer a good jumping-off point:

1. *http://global.oup.com/uk/orc/busecon/business/haberberg_rieple/01student/bibliography/#m*
2. *http://www.nickols.us/strategy_biblio.htm*
3. *https://strategyresearchinitiative.wikispaces.com/home*

I have been especially influenced by the compelling scholarship of Professor Henry Mintzberg of McGill University (*http://www.mintzberg.org/resume*), Professor Michael Porter of Harvard University (*http://www.hbs.edu/faculty/Pages/profile.aspx?facId=6532*) and Professor David Teece of the University of California at Berkeley (*http://facultybio.haas.berkeley.edu/faculty-list/teece-david*).

CHAPTER NOTES

Introduction

[1] Originally called NM Electronics.

[2] This isolation of the "failure" of competitive arbitrage is a primary assumption of the field in Economics known as Industrial Organization, which examines violations of perfect competition.

[3] This phrase was coined by Paul O'Donnell while working for me at Helmer & Associates.

[4] I very much resonate with Saloner's conclusion that perhaps the most important contribution of Game Theory to Strategic Management is "metaphorical." By metaphorical, he meant that the fundamental assumption of Game Theory—the presence of a variety of well-informed, properly motivated players, all trying to do their best—must serve as a foundational assumption. Saloner, Garth. "Modeling, Game Theory, and Strategic Management." *Strategic Management Journal* 12: Issue S2 (1991): 119–136. Print.

[5] The observed market cap would be this plus any "excess" capital (for example unneeded cash on the balance sheet), and then adjusted to reflect current levels of pricing in the stock market in order to move from absolute value to relative value. If the NPV formulation includes the initial capital needed as a negative term, then this would have to added back as well.

[6] A quick summary of FCF: *https://en.wikipedia.org/wiki/Free_cash_flow#Difference_to_net_income*

[7] There are some acceptable simplifying assumptions to derive this formula. The derivation is in Appendix 1.2. The simplifying assumptions are called out explicitly in that Appendix.

[8] Differential margins is the more important variable since, unlike market share, it is not constrained by being ≥ 0. However, there can be subtle trade-offs. For example, a

company might improve its differential margin for quite a period if it accepted steadily diminishing market share—the impact of an unprotected price umbrella.

[9] The Fundamental Formula of Strategy simplifies by assuming m and s are constants over the period in question, a hallmark of Power. Fundamental enterprise value at any point in time is the result of expectations regarding future free cash flow. As Intel moved forward in time, the prospect of withering arbitrage became clearer and the expectations for $\bar{s}$ and $\bar{m}$ changed accordingly.

[10] In developing a strategy, it is essential to not just consider existing competitors, but also potential ones. This approach has a long history in Economics as well. Baumol, William J., Panzar John C., Willig, Robert D., Bailey, Elizabeth E., Fischer, Dietrich. "Contestable Markets: An Uprising in the Theory of Industry Structure." *The American Economic Review,* Vol. 72, No. 1, (Mar., 1982): 1–15. Print.

[11] In our Chapter 3 discussion of Counter-Positioning, there is some consideration of the impact of other business units on decisions.

[12] "Not simplistic" is another term for "exhaustive." To be useful as a cognitive guide, a framework needs to cover nearly all circumstances. It is an acceptable simplification to leave out some rare occurrences. If we accept that business value is the overriding objective of any business then from the top down we know from the math that the FES, and the definitions of Power, Strategy and strategy are exhaustive. My assertion that the 7 Powers is exhaustive is of an entirely different character—it is an empirical statement. These seven have been sufficient to cover all the hundreds of cases I have dealt with as a strategy consultant and in the many cases tackled by my students, corporate and academic. It is possible that there are more than 7 Power types. Fortunately, these can simply be added on as they still have to fulfil the FES and the definition of Power. If one looks at the 7 Powers Chart, it is easy to see that the vertical dimension is exhaustive—it is simply the drivers of positive cash flow (somewhat simplified as discussed in the text). Are the four generic barriers of the horizontal dimension the only barrier types? I have thoughts on this but it is well beyond the scope of this book.

[13] I wish to thank William C. Brainard of Yale for his help in thinking through the terminal value issues in this derivation. Of course he is in no way responsible for any errors of mine.

Chapter 1

[14] The Power type here was Counter-Positioning which will be covered in Chapter 3.

[15] *http://www.webpreneurblog.com/adapt-or-die-netflix-vs-blockbuster/*

[16] Netflix also faced other competitors, such as HBO, who came at this business from a different angle, and Netflix needed Power with respect to them as well. With HBO and

similar competitors, Netflix's Power came from Counter-Positioning, which I cover in Chapter 3.

[17] To keep matters simple, the third route to improved cash flow, reduced investment needs, is not considered here.

[18] *https://finance.yahoo.com/*

[19] A *New York Times* article details some of the mistakes: *http://www.nytimes.com/2013/04/27/business/netflix-looks-back-on-its-near-death-spiral.html?pagewanted=all&_r=0*

[20] The derivation of this equation is in Appendix 1.1.

[21] In economists' terms, both are endogenous.

Chapter 2

[22] Network Economies are well-covered in the Economics literature and so my treatment will be brief. For those looking for a thoughtful exploration I recommend Shapiro, Carl, and Hal R. Varian. *Information Rules: A Strategic Guide to the Network Economy*. Boston: Harvard Business Press, 2013. Print.

[23] Source: *http://www.ere.net/2012/06/23/branchout-keeps-falling-down-down/*

[24] This formula is derived in Appendix 2.1.

[25] *http://www.forbes.com/quotes/9638/*

Chapter 3

[26] *https://www.vanguard.com/bogle_site/lib/sp19970401.html*

[27] *https://about.vanguard.com/who-we-are/a-remarkable-history/*

[28] *http://www.icifactbook.org/fb_ch2.html#popularity*

[29] Levitt, Theodore. "Marketing Myopia." *https://hbr.org/2004/07/marketing-myopia*. This is a wonderful article that has fueled long and thoughtful discussions of business definition. This capability lack is well noted in the RBV literature.

[30] Nelson, Richard R., and Sidney G. Winter. *An Evolutionary Theory of Economic Change*. Cambridge: Harvard University Press, 2009. Print.

[31] Looked at from the perspective of the FES, Disruptive Technologies tell us about the left-hand side of the equation (market scale) but tell us nothing about the right-hand side (Power).

Chapter 4

[32] *http://www.computerworld.com.au/article/542992/sap_users_rattle_sabers_over_charges_user-friendly_fiori_apps/*

[33] *http://www.amasol.com/files/sap_performance_management_-_a_trend_study_by_compuware_and_pac.pdf*

[34] *http://www.socialmediatoday.com/content/guest-post-back-popular-demand-basic-maintenance-offering-sap*

[35] *http://www.cio.com.au/article/181136/hp_supply_chain_lesson/?pp=2*

[36] *https://finance.yahoo.com/*

[37] *http://www.cio.com.au/article/181136/hp_supply_chain_lesson/*

[38] *https://finance.yahoo.com/q/hp?s=SAP+Historical+Prices*

[39] Farrell, Joseph, and Paul Klemperer. "Coordination and Lock-in: Competition with Switching Costs and Network Effects." Handbook of Industrial Organization 3 (2007): 1967–2072. Print.

[40] If the Switching Costs were created through customization/integration into the customer's business, the customer may also perceive the quality of the current product to be better than that of the competitor's. In this case, the company is able to charge a higher price for a better quality product, but competitors cannot match that quality at a competitive cost.

[41] In this book I use the term "product" to denote products and/or services.

[42] Burnham, Thomas A., Judy K. Frels and Vijay Mahajan, "Consumer Switching Costs: A Typology, Antecedents, and Consequences." *Journal of the Academy of Marketing Science*, 2003, 31:2, pp. 109–126. Print.

[43] Note the difference between relational Switching Costs and Branding: if the ability to charge a higher price because of a positive emotional valence precedes the actual owning of the good or service, this is Branding. If it comes only through experience with the product after purchase, then it is a Switching Cost. To overcome this Barrier, a challenger may need to invoke Branding Power and create a reputation for being able to create similar positive relational experiences to replace the positive valence associated with the current vendor.

[44] In Chapter 10, I will assert that the takeoff stage is the one in which Switching Costs Power needs to be established. It is this dynamic which drives that conclusion: after takeoff such arbitraging is likely to eliminate the Benefit, meaning the Power is no longer available.

[45] *https://en.wikipedia.org/wiki/List_of_SAP_products*

[46] *https://en.wikipedia.org/wiki/SAP_SE*

[47] *https://en.wikipedia.org/wiki/SAP_SE*. These are from 1991 to 2014.

[48] *https://en.wikipedia.org/wiki/SAP_SE*

Chapter 5

[49] *http://abcnews.go.com/GMA/Moms/story?id=1197202*

[50] *http://www.tiffany.com/WorldOfTiffany/TiffanyStory/Legacy/BlueBox.aspx*

[51] YCharts.com

[52] *https://finance.yahoo.com/*

[53] *http://investor.tiffany.com/releasedetail.cfm?ReleaseID=741475*

[54] Rusetski, Alexander. "The Whole New World: Nintendo's Targeting Choice." *Journal of Business Case Studies* (JBCS) 8.2 (2012): 197–212. Print.

Chapter 6

[55] *http://www.rogerebert.com/reviews/toy-story-1995*

[56] *http://boxofficequant.com/23/ from data from www.the-numbers.com*

[57] The box office relative to a film's cost gives an indication of the profitability of a film. Of course this chart is domestic box office only and does not include revenue sources other than theatrical release.

[58] From a personal correspondence with Hamilton Helmer.

[59] Price, D. A. (2008). *The Pixar Touch: The Making of a Company*. New York: Alfred A. Knopf, p. 107. Print.

[60] If there were many repeats of the Brad Bird experience—a proven director finding commercial success for the first time by joining Pixar—then one might argue that there is a deeper cause at work. But, so far, the Brad Bird experience has been idiosyncratic and hence does not lead to such conclusions.

Chapter 7

[61] *https://en.wikipedia.org/wiki/Ford_River_Rouge_Complex*

[62] *http://www.inboundlogistics.com/cms/article/the-evolution-of-inbound-logistics-the-ford-and-toyota-legacy-origin-of-the-species/*

[63] *http://www.thehenryford.org/exhibits/modelt/pdf/ModelTHeritageSelfGuidedTour_hfm.pdf*

[64] *https://en.wikipedia.org/wiki/Planned_obsolescence*

[65] *The Economist*, July 17, 2015, "Hypercars and Hyperbole."

[66] Spear, Steven, and H. Kent Bowen. "Decoding the DNA of the Toyota Production System." *Harvard Business Review* 77, no. 5 (September–October 1999): 96–106. Print.

[67] *http://www.thisamericanlife.org/radio-archives/episode/403/transcript*

[68] *https://finance.yahoo.com/*

[69] Strategic Management to the academic community.

[70] Porter, M. E. "What Is Strategy?" *Harvard Business Review* 74, no. 6 (November–December 1996): 61–78. Print.

[71] As noted earlier, when I turn to strategy Dynamics, operational excellence can be vitally important for certain Power types.

[72] Argote, L., and D. Epple. "Learning Curves in Manufacturing." Science 247.4945 (1990): 920–24. Web.

[73] In this case, each company would exhibit a similarly sloped Experience Curve parallel to each other and horizontally displaced by their difference in "Experience."

[74] Simon, Herbert A. "Bounded Rationality and Organizational Learning." Organization Science 2.1 (1991): 125–34. Web.

[75] Hughes, Jonathan R.T. "Fact and Theory in Economic History." Explorations in Economic History 3, no.2 (1966): 75–101. Print.

[76] Prahalad, Coimbatore K. "The Role of Core Competencies in the Corporation." Research Technology Management 36.6 (1993): 40. Print.

Chapter 8

[77] "Power = Benefit + Barrier" is open-ended and exhaustive. My view that the 7 Powers of this book are exhaustive is an empirical statement: these seven cover every strategy assignment I have undertaken in my career as well as every situation my students have researched. However, should more Power types emerge, they can simply be added on. Whatever their character, they must satisfy the Benefit + Barrier requirement; otherwise $\overline{m}$ in the Fundamental Equation of Strategy will not be materially positive, and hence value will not result.

[78] *http://www.inc.com/magazine/20051201/qa-hastings.html*

[79] *Ibid.*

[80] *http://techcrunch.com/2011/01/27/streaming-subscriber-growth-netflix*

[81] *http://allthingsd.com/20100810/its-official-epix-netflix-announce-multi-year-deal-for-streaming-movies/*

[82] *http://deadline.com/2011/03/netflix-to-enter-original-programming-with-mega-deal-for-david-fincher-kevin-spacey-drama-series-house-of-cards-114184/*

83 *http://www.nytimes.com/2015/04/20/business/media/netflix-is-betting-its-future-on-exclusive-programming.html?_r=0*

84 *https://en.wikipedia.org/wiki/List_of_original_programs_distributed_by_Netflix*

85 *https://finance.yahoo.com/*

86 Mintzberg, Henry. *Crafting Strategy*. Boston, MA: Harvard Business School Press, 1987: 65–75. Print.

87 Porter, Michael E. "Towards a Dynamic Theory of Strategy." Strat. Mgmt. J. Strategic Management Journal 12.S2 (1991): 95-117. Web.

88 In Chapter 1 I used the economist's term "endogenous" in reference to Industry Economics, meaning that the business could itself influence this as opposed to considering it beyond their span of control. Streaming is a good example of this. Netflix changed the Industry Economics—those conditions faced by all players.

89 The arrows in my diagram have dotted outlines to indicate possibility as opposed to guarantee: resources + changed external circumstances may or may not lead to invention and invention may or may not lead to Power. Netflix could have easily decided not to enter streaming. Or they could have entered streaming but fumbled the originals ball.

90 Bob Manz, my thoughtful partner in Helmer & Associates, coined this term.

91 Unlike prior discussions in this book, value in this context pertains to the value to the customer not the value to the offering company. However, we fulfill the value to the company requirement of the Benefit by including in the definition of compelling value the condition that pricing is such that attractive margins are realized.

92 Grove, Andrew S. *Only The Paranoid Survive*. New York: Currency Doubleday, 1996. Print.

93 Hamilton Helmer interview with Bob Wulff of Adobe.

94 *Business Week,* May 25, 1998 as cited in http://archive.wired.com/gadgets/mac/commentary/cultofmac/2006/03/70512?currentPage=all

95 Hecht, Jeff. *City of Light: The Story of Fiber Optics*. New York: Oxford UP, 1999. 139. Print.

96 I interviewed Dr. Schultz on this invention. Peter still has a large sample of this historic pull at his home in St. Thomas!

97 Nathan, John. *Sony: The Extraordinary Story behind the People and the Products*. London: HarperCollinsBusiness, 1999. 304. Print.

98 Burgelman, Robert A., and Grove, Andrew S. *Strategy Is Destiny: How Strategy-Making Shapes a Company's Future*. New York: Free, 2002. Print.

99 Alpha is the returns above those from just investing in "the market" after appropriate adjustment for risk.

[100] This 22-year period encompasses both periods when my equity investing was for proprietary accounts and for Strategy Capital. There were two periods I exited public equities entirely and these are not included. Their inclusion would have increased my returns relative to the benchmark as the entry and exit decisions were favorably timed.

[101] Of course this compounding adds up. Over the investing period, my portfolio increased 615.9 times versus 12.1 times for the S&P500TR.

[102] My portfolio is unlevered.

[103] This probability is an assessment of draws: "For all draws across the investment period 1994–2015, what share of the draws failed to outperform the market for different hold periods?"

[104] Another similarly revealing pairing is IBM's mainframe business versus its PC business, the first having Power and the second not.

Chapter 9

[105] For those wishing to learn more, I recommend *The Intel Trinity*. My brief narrative on Intel draws heavily on this fine study by Michael Malone. Malone, Michael. *The Intel Trinity: How Noyce, Moore, and Grove Built the World's Most Important Company*. HarperBusiness, 2015. Print.

[106] *https://en.wikipedia.org/wiki/IBM_Personal_Computer*

[107] *https://finance.yahoo.com/*

[108] I want to express my appreciation to Wally Rhines, the CEO of Mentor Graphics, and Bill Mitchell of Gemfinder and Mitchell Capital for their acute analysis of Intel's sources of Power.

[109] In a personal correspondence with Hamilton Helmer.

[110] *http://jeremyreimer.com/m-item.lsp?i=137*

[111] It is possible for Cornered Resources to come into play after origination. For example, certain process innovations achieved at a later stage might either be patented or kept as trade secrets. However, most of these tend to fail the test of significance. They are usually incremental in their contribution to returns, as the fundamental positions have often been arbitraged out much earlier.

[112] If a market is large, the scaling may have been so extensive during the takeoff phase that such complexity/opacity might be achieved.

[113] This quality also underlies the investment results discussed in Appendix 9.1.

ABOUT THE AUTHOR

Hamilton Helmer has spent his career as a practicing business strategist. At Helmer & Associates (later Deep Strategy), a strategy consulting firm he founded, he has led over 200 strategy projects with major clients such as Adobe Systems, Agilent Technologies, Coursera, Hewlett-Packard, John Hancock Mutual Life, Mentor Graphics, Netflix, Raychem, and Spotify. In the last two decades he has also utilized his Strategy concepts as an active equity investor and is currently Chief Investment Officer and Co-Founder of Strategy Capital. Prior to Helmer & Associates he was employed at Bain & Company. He holds a Ph.D. in Economics from Yale University and is a Phi Beta Kappa graduate of Williams College. Mr. Helmer just retired as Chairman of the Board of American Science and Engineering (NASDAQ: ASEI) and currently teaches Business Strategy in the Economics Department of Stanford University.

More information may be found at *www.7powers.com*.

44539909R00130

Made in the USA
San Bernardino, CA
17 January 2017